HOW TO ANALYZE PEOPLE & MIND MANIPULATION FOR BEGINNERS

2 Books in 1: Learn Everything about Persuasion, Mind Control, How to Influence People and Manage Your Emotions

Jenifer Thompson

© Copyright 2020 by Jenifer Thompson. All right reserved.

The work contained herein has been produced with the intent to provide relevant knowledge and information on the topic on the topic described in the title for entertainment purposes only. While the author has gone to every extent to furnish up to date and true information, no claims can be made as to its accuracy or validity as the author has made no claims to be an expert on this topic. Notwithstanding, the reader is asked to do their own research and consult any subject matter experts they deem necessary to ensure the quality and accuracy of the material presented herein.

This statement is legally binding as deemed by the Committee of Publishers Association and the American Bar Association for the territory of the United States. Other jurisdictions may apply their own legal statutes. Any reproduction, transmission or copying of this material contained in this work without the express written consent of the copyright holder shall be deemed as a copyright violation as per the current legislation in force on the date of publishing and subsequent time thereafter. All additional works derived from this material may be claimed by the holder of this copyright.

The data, depictions, events, descriptions and all other information forthwith are considered to be true, fair and accurate unless the work is expressly described as a work of fiction. Regardless of the nature of this work, the Publisher is exempt from any responsibility of actions taken by the reader in conjunction with this work. The Publisher acknowledges that the reader acts of their own accord and releases the author and Publisher of any responsibility for the observance of tips, advice, counsel, strategies and techniques that may be offered in this volume.

TABLE OF CONTENTS

MIND MANIPULATION FOR BEGINNERS
Learn How To Influence People And Manage Your Emotions Through Persuasion And Mind Control

Introduction 3
Chapter 1 *What Is Mind Manipulation?* 5
Chapter 2 *Is Mind Manipulation Ethical?* 10
Chapter 3 *Influence, Don't Be Influenced* 13
Chapter 4 *The Influence Of Language* 18
Chapter 5 *Building Strong Rapport* 21
Chapter 6 *Do The Thinking For Them* 24
Chapter 7 *Use The Snowball Effect* 27
Chapter 8 *Receive An Inch, Take A Mile* 30
Chapter 9 *Your Real Deadline Is Not Your Declared Deadline* 34
Chapter 10 *Give More Than You Take* 37
Chapter 11 *Stand For Something Big* 42
Chapter 12 *Be Shameless* 45
Chapter 13 *The Power Of Body Language* 49
Chapter 14 *Use Redirections As Often As Needed* 53
Chapter 15 *Research People And Get To Know Them* 56
Chapter 16 *Right Timing, Right Opportunity* 60
Chapter 17 *Expand Your Mind Power* 64
Chapter 18 *Always Have A Positive Desire* 68
Conclusion 72
Description 74

HOW TO ANALYZE PEOPLE
Learn How to Read People by Analyzing Body Language, Behavioral Psychology and Emotional Intelligence

Introduction 78
Chapter 1 *Why Analyze People?* 79
Chapter 2 *Get To Know Body Language* 82

Chapter 3 *Facial Expressions Speak Volumes*..86

Chapter 4 *The Fbi's Method For Eye Analysis*..89

Chapter 5 *Trust Your Intuition* 91

Chapter 6 *Become Aware Of Emotional Energy*..95

Chapter 7 *Develop Your Baseline Understanding* 99

Chapter 8 *Pay Close Attention To People Deviating Away*............................. 103

Chapter 9 *Beware Of Cluster Gestures*.. 109

Chapter 10 *Compare And Contrast What You Discover*.................................113

Chapter 11 *Observe Mirrored Behaviors* 117

Chapter 12 *Identify The Strong Voice*..121

Chapter 13 *Pay Attention To Their Walk* 126

Chapter 14 *Be Aware Of Action Words* 130

Chapter 15 *Be Aware Of Personality Clues*... 134

Chapter 16 *Never Forget To Put It Together!* 139

Chapter 17 *Make Your Guess And Validate It*.. 142

Chapter 18 *Be Flexible In Your Understanding* 146

Conclusion 149

Description... 151

MIND MANIPULATION FOR BEGINNERS

Learn How To Influence People And Manage Your Emotions Through Persuasion And Mind Control

Jenifer Thompson

© Copyright 2020 by Jenifer Thompson. All right reserved.

The work contained herein has been produced with the intent to provide relevant knowledge and information on the topic on the topic described in the title for entertainment purposes only. While the author has gone to every extent to furnish up to date and true information, no claims can be made as to its accuracy or validity as the author has made no claims to be an expert on this topic. Notwithstanding, the reader is asked to do their own research and consult any subject matter experts they deem necessary to ensure the quality and accuracy of the material presented herein.

This statement is legally binding as deemed by the Committee of Publishers Association and the American Bar Association for the territory of the United States. Other jurisdictions may apply their own legal statutes. Any reproduction, transmission or copying of this material contained in this work without the express written consent of the copyright holder shall be deemed as a copyright violation as per the current legislation in force on the date of publishing and subsequent time thereafter. All additional works derived from this material may be claimed by the holder of this copyright.

The data, depictions, events, descriptions and all other information forthwith are considered to be true, fair and accurate unless the work is expressly described as a work of fiction. Regardless of the nature of this work, the Publisher is exempt from any responsibility of actions taken by the reader in conjunction with this work. The Publisher acknowledges that the reader acts of their own accord and releases the author and Publisher of any responsibility for the observance of tips, advice, counsel, strategies and techniques that may be offered in this volume.

INTRODUCTION

Congratulations on purchasing *Mind Manipulation for Beginners!* This book is your brand new go-to guide for learning everything you need to know about marketing so that you can take your life and your business to the next level.

Before we dive deep into the concepts of mind manipulation, I want to unpack two critical discussions. The first is *"what." What* are you marketing? In other words, why do you need to learn about mind manipulation? If you are running a business, selling a product, or offering services for sale, you will need excellent marketing skills to get yourself out there. Even if you are not doing any of the activities above, you still need to know how to market. In this case, you are selling yourself. You might be marketing yourself to your boss, friends, family, and people who can offer you a desirable opportunity, or even your community. Marketing yourself could be for anything from wanting to have the "in" on new career opportunities and want to hold a specific reputation with the people around you. No matter what you desire, knowing how to market yourself is an essential skill.

An excellent sales mentor once told me that there is no such thing as sales skills. Instead, those that are great at selling are excellent at *believing in themselves*. They have such massive confidence that, no matter what they do, they are excellent at it because people are always attracted to their energy. This is precisely what we will cover, which leads me to the second point I want to make before we dig in.

Why mind "manipulation?" Isn't "manipulation" an ugly word? Won't you find yourself walking in a grey zone of "good vs. bad?" I understand why you might have that concern, but I want to assure you that this book is about none of that. Manipulation, at its core, is the practice of managing or influencing, skillfully. If you have ill intentions, you are likely to manipulate someone poorly. If you have positive intentions, you can use your skills to influence others' in a productive way. How you root your intention is how you approach the process of mind manipulation, so it is worthwhile to root yourself in a positive, service-oriented space before you begin marketing. This way, you have a positive impact on others' lives, you empower people to experience excellence, and you promote yourself in a way that works toward creating the best possible outcome for everyone involved.

Anytime you are in a promotion position, whether you are promoting yourself, a company, a product, a service, or anything else, your number one objective is always to find people who want to say "yes" to what you are offering. Mind manipulation, then, is about learning how to speak in a way that the people you know would benefit most from your offer are inclined to say "yes." You know that many people would benefit significantly from what you have available at your core. You just need to get them to see that. Then, mind manipulation is about becoming an empowering influencer that encourages everyone to tap into their greatness as profoundly as possible.

Suppose you are ready to discover how you can maximize your influence, promote positive solutions to others, and expand your sales skills through your ability to communicate your confidence. In that case, you are ready to dive into *Mind Manipulation for Beginners!* Let's get started!

CHAPTER 1
What Is Mind Manipulation?

When you picture sales, do you ever find yourself plagued by horrific images of used car salespeople that use deceit and confusion to push their products on people who genuinely do not need them? This stereotype has been plastered over people that typically sell vacuums, appliances, furniture, and even cell phones and other technology. The root of the stereotype is based on outdated sales techniques that intentionally deceive someone into believing they needed something when, in fact, they didn't. It was an entirely self-serving experience where the salesperson was more focused on their sale than the other individual's real need. These days, this sales approach is rarely used, partly because most people can see right through it, and partially because this is a crummy form of mind manipulation that you *do not* want to use. Yes, it may lead to sales. *However,* people will eventually catch on, and you will lose your reputation in the process, which means your long-term gains will be compromised.

Don't Be the Used Car Salesman

The stereotypical used car salesman could sell snow to a ski hill in the middle of a thriving winter. They are *excellent* in sales and can turn results, and there's no doubting that. The trouble with this sales approach is that, in the end, they turn out many customers that walk away feeling the dreaded buyers' remorse. When a buyer walks away feeling displeased with their purchase in any way, whatsoever, they associate that feeling with the salesperson. *Then what?*
Their customers don't think highly of their experience with that salesman. They leave negative reviews, complain openly, and don't refer to anyone. Mostly, they begin to recognize that person as being someone they cannot trust. As a salesperson, regardless of whether you are promoting a company or yourself, you *never* want to be associated with someone that uses shady sales tactics and cannot be trusted. This behavior will catch up with you and stop you in your tracks, leaving you unable to create any sort of long-term success for yourself.
Rather than being the stereotypical salesperson that sells buyer's remorse, you need to be the salesperson that sells a pleasant experience that is talked about for years to come. This is done by focusing less on your bottom line and more on your client. There are four stages in which this will happen: the approach, the warm-up, the pitch, and the sale.
The approach could be cold, warm, or hot. During a cold sale, you are generally the one approaching a client who has no idea who you are, what you have to offer, or why you are coming to them. These approaches are most challenging, as you have to get that individual warm, then hot,

before pitching and selling. With warm approaches, the client is already interested and is looking for you to give them a reason to say yes, and with hot approaches, your client has already said yes and is ready to finalize the sale.

During the warm-up, your objective is to bring someone from cold to hot, so you can comfortably pitch and make a sale. This is where you get to make a difference and create an approach that leaves a positive, lasting impression. The tacky, stereotypical approach would be to fish for knowledge that you could use to manipulate that person into buying what you want them to buy, rather than what they need. Again, this might land you an immediate sale, but it will lose you a loyal fan, which is far more valuable. The better approach is to get to know your client, so you can offer them a solution that fits their specific needs, which means you land an immediate sale and gain a loyal fan that will send all their friends in your direction. In some cases, the quick sale may have less face value, but a devoted fan's long-term benefit is far more valuable.

The pitch in a stereotypical car salesman type approach is where you would use all of the information you have learned to push someone into buying the most expensive thing you can manipulate on them. In a positive approach, this is where you tailor one of your solutions to meet their needs so you can offer them something they genuinely want *and* need. In traditional sales, this is where you decide what product or service will fit them best and get them ready to say "yes" to it. If you are selling yourself to build your network, this is where you decide how you can fit into someone else's network, so they welcome you in happily.

The sale is where you make your ask. The ask is often the most challenging part, as this is where people fear they will be rejected, and a fear of rejection is *severe*. The fear of rejection can lead to you getting turned down and missing out on commissions, sales targets, and promotions in sales. In your personal life, fear of rejection can lead to you not getting someone else's number, being rejected into someone's network, or being rejected from a community you wanted to be a part of. Each of us has a history that makes rejection feel painful and intimidating, which is why your fear of being rejected is entirely natural, and this response is widespread. However, you cannot let it get the best of you. You must learn how to make your ask so that people have the opportunity to say "yes" to whatever you are offering, whether it be a product or service, or friendship, or even a date.

Get to YOUR "Yes" First

If you are already focused on getting *them* to say yes, you need to slow down. You should never focus on getting someone else to say yes before you have said yes within yourself. Every successful sale starts with you because, at the end of the day, *you* are what people are paying for. To understand what I mean, think back to a product that you considered buying for quite a while before you finally made your purchase. Though you knew about the product for some time, you were not ready to purchase it until you finally chose to go for it. What changed between the time you bought and all the other times you were exposed to the product? *The person that was offering it to you.*

People often think that a sales rejection comes from genuinely not having the money or desire for a product. The reality is, if someone stopped long enough to learn about what a product was and discover its price, they are interested. It's not funds or desire that prevents them from purchasing. It's the person offering the product that stops them. If you have been in sales for any period, this may be challenging to accept, but it is true. People buy from people they like. That time you finally made the purchase, the only thing that changed was the person selling it to you. They made the experience enjoyable to the point where you finally said, "yes." Even if it was the same person selling to you, something about *that* experience ultimately sold you on the product, hence the change.

To become masterful at selling products, services, or yourself, you need to get to your own "yes" first. You need to feel confident in three things: yourself, your offer, and the recipient. Without confidence in these three areas, you will struggle immensely to have any impact on others, which will make it seemingly impossible to sell anything to anyone, no matter how well-fit it may be for that person.

With yourself, you need to feel confident that your personality aligns with the offer and the person you are selling to. You should feel sure that you are offering from a place you genuinely believe in, that you deserve to make such an offer, and that you are capable of providing something positive and life-changing for the other person. Develop confidence in your ability to say the right things, talk to the right people, and make the right offers, as this confidence will transfer into the conversations you have with your leads.

With your offer, you must stand behind it. No matter what you are offering, you need to genuinely believe that it has value to the people you are selling it to and that their lives will be positively impacted. If you are new to sales, you might have to be selective at first to pick something that you already genuinely believe in, as this takes away the need to build a belief in your product. Over time, however, you will discover that you can begin to genuinely believe in just about anything you desire to sell, unless it specifically goes against your values, in which case you should never sell it. For everything else, you will have to look for a way to find value in it, so you can feel confident in making that offer to someone else.

With your recipient, you must know you have chosen the right person. Sure, you could sell anything to anyone, but remember, you do *not* want to create buyer's remorse. You need to create a specific avatar in your mind that represents the type of person who would best benefit from your offer and then focus on selling to that type of person. No matter what avatar you have chosen, you will find an abundance of people that are perfectly suited to your offer. *Those* are the people you want to look for, build rapport with, and sell to *after* you have already developed confidence in yourself and your offer.

Sell From the Mindset Out

If you want to maximize your impact on mind manipulation, you need to sell from the mindset out. Your focus should be on what you believe and how you feel, on the applicable offer, and then on the person you are selling to. This way, everything you do is rooted in attraction-based marketing, rather than pushy marketing strategies. If you are marketing a product or service, first you need to believe in yourself and your ability to make that offer, then you need to believe in the product or service, then you need to believe in the client. If you are marketing a relationship with yourself, you first have to believe in yourself and your worthiness. In the functional connection, and then in the person you are offering it to. No matter what you are marketing, you need to create this inside-out approach so that, when the time comes, you are selling from a firm foundation. This way, nothing rocks you from your deep sense of belief in yourself and what you are doing, and that deep-seated confidence makes the sale for you.

If you are currently in a sales position and are reading this book to master your ability to make a sale, I want you to step away from your sales objective for the time being. If you are currently looking to attract more people into your network and are selling yourself, I want you to step away from your networking objective for a few minutes. Before you can master any of that, you need to master *you*. When you feel worthy of showing up in front of someone, talking to them, and receiving something from them, everything falls into place. People notice when someone is confident, believes in themselves, and can see their self-worth and deservingness. They pay attention, listen closer, and are more likely to oblige anything they are offering. If you can create *that* foundation, you can sell anything. Cement your foundation of self-belief using the following three approaches: perception, alter ego, and discipline. With your perception, get honest with yourself about why you do anything in life. What is your bottom line in your overall life, and how does that drive you to make decisions and take action? What values do you hold? Clarify who you are, what you want, and why you want it, then tell yourself a story that creates a positive perception around yourself, your desires, and your motives.

Alter egos are an excellent way to create distance between yourself and your desires so you can clarify the information as mentioned above with ease. You can also use your alter ego to step away from false stories you have been telling yourself, or fears you have been feeding yourself with, to immediately step into excellence. For example, if you have previously said to yourself that sales are tacky and manipulative and that there is no such thing as an "honest" salesperson, develop an alter ego for yourself that believes otherwise. Create a persona that believes in honest sales, values honesty in every sale they make, and embodies that persona as frequently as possible, especially when making sales.

Discipline is essential when it comes to any form of personal growth or achievement. With discipline, you can hold to your values, maintain your honest perception and discard false perceptions, and embody your alter ego as needed. You can also drive yourself to learn more, do more, and become more to satisfy your goals. When you implement self-discipline in your life, you take charge and become the boss of your experience, where deep-rooted confidence comes from. Once you have that, you can achieve anything you desire, including mind manipulation.

CHAPTER 2
Is Mind Manipulation Ethical?

I want to stress the importance of using manipulative powers *positively*. I am not here to teach you how to get anything you want from anyone you want, as doing so would ultimately prove to be unfulfilling and even harmful to the person you are manipulating, and yourself. Knowing how to use manipulation ethically ensures that you reach your objectives without harming anyone in the process, which is essential if you want to embody these skills powerfully.

Detach From the Outcome

An excellent way to ensure that your manipulation strategies remain ethical is to detach from the outcome. People who stay attached to a specific result, such as desiring fulfillment from a particular person, find themselves engaging in unhealthy manipulation because they attempt to force the situation with that individual. It may seem as though you *must* gain your desired result from that person, but this is entirely untrue. The reality is, that person does not have to be a part of you fulfilling your desires, and it is perfectly fine if they are not. Rather than fixating on anyone, fixate on your desired outcome and be open to creating that outcome with anyone who deems themselves the right person to create that outcome.

Let's say you want to sell an annual membership to your new gym, for example. You could try forcing that sale on anyone that walks through the door using manipulative sales tactics, which would inevitably lead to a negative reputation for your gym. Or, you could wait for the *right* person to come through the door. The person who was already eager to exercise felt excited about your gym's offerings and felt sure they would make use of the membership to be a far more valuable sale than anyone else. Why? Because that person is the perfect fit, they will bring others who are also an ideal fit. Thus, a stream of perfect-fit-clients would be coming through your door in no time, and the reputation of your gym would grow as you were routinely booked out and filled with excellent clients.

Detaching from the outcome does not mean that you give up on creating your desired results. Instead, it means keeping yourself open to connecting with the right people, so you can make the right offer at the right time and land the deal. This way, you refrain from manipulating ill-fit people into positions they do not need to be in. Instead, they focus on creating an excellent environment for the best-fit people only.

Always Respect the Other

You will inevitably come across people who are an excellent fit for your offer and people who are not an ideal fit. Having the right perspective around each individual you meet ensures you are always ethically using mind manipulation, primarily because you are focused on respecting the other person.

If you meet someone that is an ill fit for your offer, it is not respectful nor kind to blatantly ignore that person or treat them in an unkind manner because they cannot benefit you. Doing this would be a sign of malicious manipulation, and it can also negatively affect your reputation. Although this person may not fit your offer, they still deserve to receive positive, respectful interactions from you. Further, they might know someone that would be an excellent fit for your recommendation, and they would be far more likely to refer that person to you if they, themselves, had a positive experience with you. At the very least, you do not want them telling everyone else you have a poor attitude because those who receive your positive attitude will begin to wonder if you are faking it for sale.

When you meet someone that is an excellent fit for your offer, it may seem like you *have* to find a way to get that person to see it that way. If that person is already inclined to say yes, go with the flow and make the sale. Should that person be hesitant, resistant, or outright against your offer, you must respectfully navigate this. Your specific approach will depend on how they respond, and it should happen in a way that encourages them to see the best in the opportunity without making them feel forced to take any action on it.

For someone that is mildly hesitant or resistant toward your offer, but who does not express that they are outright against it, you want to *stop asking*. The more you ask, the more inclined a client will be to say no. As well, the less ethical you become because you are no longer respecting their right to take their time or say no. You *must* respect their right to think about it, ask questions, and take the time to earn their trust and their "yes." Rather than asking questions, learn more in-depth into the "warming up" phase by getting to know them more, building a positive connection, and exposing them to your offer without pressuring them around it. Do not make any further offers until they express interest in your request once again, then make the offer.

If someone is entirely against what you are offering, you must strictly follow the steps mentioned above. Do not discuss anything relating to your offer even further, not even your testimony or results with that product or service. Instead, focus exclusively on building a connection with them and earning their trust. As you build positive rapport, they will pay closer attention to you and will inevitably learn about your offer through social media, overheard conversations, and word of mouth from others'. Over time, they may come back and ask you about it, in which case you have the opportunity to make the offer again. Never make the offer before that; otherwise, you disrespect that person's right to say no, and they *will not trust you*. Attempting to force someone to say "yes" or rush through their decision is a clear sign of disrespect, and this is where you start to fall into the non-ethical mind manipulation tactics that are not worth the reputation they'll cost you.

Work for the Good of All

An effortless way to guarantee that you remain ethical in your approach is to always work for the good of all. When you value respect, honesty, transparency, right to choose, and the highest interest of all, you know you are working from a position of ethical manipulation. In this case, your focus is less on controlling others to do something and more on manipulating yourself to be the type of person others want to say "yes" to. This way, you are attracting others to your offer by always creating a positive, respectful, enjoyable experience for anyone that comes across you.

CHAPTER 3
Influence, Don't Be Influenced

Influencers have become one of the most talked-about industries in recent years. As consumers spend more time online, influencers have sprung up as representatives for a variety of companies. Essentially, they are responsible for encouraging you to take a specific action, especially when connecting you with a product or brand they think you might like. Generally speaking, they have done many beautiful things for online industries. Operating in all areas of interest, influencers can earn an audience's respect and trust and use that to sell to their audience effortlessly. Each of us has been influenced in one way or another, likely by major influencers, too. However, it is not just professional influencers that monopolize their relationship with you to earn their desired outcome. Friends, family, coworkers, bosses, colleagues, politicians, salespeople, and many other everyday people are also using their influence to encourage you to make confident choices or behave in a specific way.

If you are aware of the influence others' have over you, and you take the time to think critically and make the right choice for you and them, influence is not a big deal. Most of us are not being consciously influenced, though, which leads to us making choices without clearly understanding why or how these choices affect us or anyone else. If you want to become masterful at the art of mind manipulation, you have to learn how to influence rather than be influenced.

Why You Need to Stop Being Influenced

Being unconsciously influenced by the world around you inevitably leads to you taking actions and making choices that may be an ill fit for you. This is where those that might use mind manipulation in a negative, harmful manner can penetrate and dissuade you from the things you truly desire in life. For example, people could influence you to stop trying, hold back from taking meaningful action or give up on something you want. They could also influence you to follow a completely different path from what you genuinely desire, which creates room for trouble.

Rather than being influenced by others and finding yourself on the wrong path, or no path at all, you need to learn to release others' control over you. It is okay to be influenced as long as you aim to be consciously influenced. In other words, recognize when someone is attempting to affect you, critically question their intentions, and decide if their influence aligns with what you genuinely want for yourself. One thing to be cautious about is that if it *does* align with what you want, but the person offering it is attempting to manipulate you in an unkind manner, you should refuse the offer from that person. Instead, look for someone that can make the same offer while also respecting you and giving you the freedom to make your own choices. In other words, find someone to sell to you the same way you aspire to sell to others, with respect, enthusiasm, and concern for their genuine need.

The Art of Influence Lies Within YOU

Mind manipulation and influence starts with you. Amateur influencers attempt to influence others by focusing entirely on that person, and not enough on themselves. You must concentrate on influencing through attraction rather than force. In other words, you want to lead people to follow you, rather than herd them in your desired direction. Focusing entirely on yourself, your energy, and how you can attract people toward you, rather than others', their needs, and how you can drive them to do what you want, is where the real power of influence lies.

An excellent way to understand where the power of influence lies is to think about your favorite influencer and consider how they do business. Are they chasing people, pushing sales on people, and attempting to force people to take their offers? Not likely. Instead, they are genuinely enjoying their lives, promoting positivity, celebrating others, and sharing offers that they believe can improve others' lives. Through this, people became attracted to them and are influenced by what they are doing. Thus they become effective influencers.

Influence By Believing In Yourself

The level to which you believe in yourself directly correlates to how you can influence others. People are not led by those that resist believing in themselves, lack confidence in who they are, and show up with fear. Leaders that lack self-belief and confidence fail to lead because they cannot generate feelings of security, certainty, and direction in their audience. Rather than offering answers that followers are looking for, they are asking questions.

Believing in yourself enough to manipulate others to follow your influence requires you to follow a two-layered approach that will drastically build your belief in yourself and others' confidence in you, as well. First, you must believe in yourself. Next, you must believe in your offer.

To believe in yourself, you must first understand who you are and what you stand for. Identify your values, morals, and personal beliefs, and approach everything in a way that allows you to uphold these necessary guiding stones in your life. Believe sincerely that you are capable of fulfilling your values, morals, and beliefs in everything you do, and that you always stand behind things that serve you and those around you. When you believe that you are always serving from a place of good, leading others with gratitude, and adding to the world's positivity, it becomes easier to believe in yourself. As you believe in yourself, others see that level of self-belief and are far more likely to follow you and pay attention to what you have to offer.

To believe in your offer, whether it be a product, service, friendship, or anything else, you must believe that it genuinely can benefit the other person. Look to observe that offer in a way that makes it clear that it can add value to someone else's life, and always get into that point of genuine belief before ever making the offer. This means you need to take time to believe in the offer overall and to believe in how that offer will benefit a specific individual so that you feel confident and comfortable offering it to them. For example, let's say you are selling home security devices. Everyone can benefit from a home security device because it provides them with a sense of protection and safety within their own home, which is easy to believe in. Now, you have to see how that would matter to a specific client you are looking to sell to. Perhaps they are a single mom, an older person, or someone who is not home often. Therefore, they need the device for added protection. Understanding how it benefits them, specifically, allows you to believe deeply enough in your offer to make it and sell it to the other person.

To be clear, your level of belief matters because it turns you into a *leader*. You are no longer asking questions or seeking permission from others. Instead, you are permitting yourself and giving others' the consent they need to make the choices they wish to make, too. Permission marketing is achieved only by genuinely believing in yourself. People feel your level of confidence and authority and take your permission seriously anytime you make them an offer.

Be Genuine In Who You Are

We have all come across an influencer that was not genuine at one time or another. You know the type the moment you see those influencers, too. They exude an energy that seems off or out of touch, and they are challenging to relate to. It appears as though these influencers are living in their own world, and not in a world they genuinely believe in or enjoy being a part of, either. Instead, they are living in a world that seems manufactured to force others' to believe something about that individual, as though they are trying to hide who they indeed are. Those types of influencers never make it in the industry, as an unrealistic experience overshadows their longevity that even they cannot genuinely believe in.

If you want to have a significant, lasting impact on others, you need to influence them from the point of authenticity. You must be true to who you are, show up as your genuine self, and speak authentically to your audience. Tell the truth, be bold in your personality, and own your flaws and strengths with confidence. Be confident in your "human" self.

When you operate from being truly aligned with who you are, confidence, self-belief, and momentum grow effortlessly. Rather than trying to force confidence or belief in something that feels ill-fit for you, or attempting to push yourself in a direction you do not particularly care about, you flow with ease. This ease conveys into everything you say and do and goes a long way toward developing success with your influential abilities and your mind manipulation success.

Show Interest and Be Helpful

Here is where you get to start focusing on others. An effective salesperson executing modern mind manipulation techniques will not focus on forcing others to make their desired choices. Instead, they show interest and offer help in a meaningful way. Their focus is less on "What can I get from you?" and more on "How can I support you?" No matter what industry you are working in, your audience wants and needs your support. Remember, followers have questions, leaders have answers. Your followers want you to encourage them to ask questions, as they are often afraid to come to you themselves. They don't want to waste your time, interrupt you, or feel like they are drawing attention to themselves. If you willingly offer that attention, they feel confident and safe, asking their pending questions. You also gain the opportunity to answer them and offer solutions. Thus, you create a situation where your follower feels empowered, and you gain the opportunity to make your offer.

The key to showing interest and being helpful is to do it in as many ways as possible, not just regarding the sale you want to make. Showing interest in your followers as a whole person shows that you genuinely care about them and how you can support them, and not just how they can support you. Offer small things relevant to them, even if they are not directly associated with your big offer. For example, offer knowledge or information for how they could have a better experience with something in their lives. When people see you as helpful and realize that your help actually creates positive results in their lives, they trust you more. As they trust you more, they come to you with additional questions and become far more likely to respond positively to your offer.

Exude Positive, Welcoming Energy

The energy you put out is the energy you receive back, and the most expansive energy there is – positive energy. When you maintain a cheerful, optimistic outlook on life, you become far more enjoyable to be around because you promote energy that people want to be a part of. *Everyone* can use more happiness in their lives.

Smiling is an excellent way to combine positive, welcoming energy. A genuine smile is always more valuable than a fake smile, so learn to cheer yourself up, so each smile is authentic and cheerful. The most beautiful aspect of a smile is that smiles are free to offer, and they rapidly lift anyone's mood. You never know who desperately needs that smile, or who can benefit the most from it. When you become a cheerful, happy face that people look forward to seeing, you maximize your influence over others.

To become more welcoming, focus on mindfully inviting anyone into your circle. Make everyone feel included, be respectful to anyone that may be a part of your audience, or be associated with your audience and provide a connection for those that seek it. People love being a part of something that feels good, and that makes them feel as though they belong, so if you can create that energy within yourself, you will increase your influential abilities and learn mind manipulation.

CHAPTER 4
The Influence Of Language

Language is a superpower. The words you say communicate specific messages, both explicitly and subliminally. Some messages people will receive on the surface, while others will be shared directly to their subconscious mind. Knowing how to use subliminal messaging to communicate with the subconscious mind is an excellent way to get people to see the value in you and your opportunity.

There are plenty of excellent ways that you can communicate to someone's subconscious mind without playing in the gray or off-limit areas of mind manipulation. Using these methods to your advantage supports you with creating your desired outcome in a way that remains positive and enjoyable for the person you are selling to.

Speak Intelligently

The way you speak matters. Leaders do not mumble, ask for permission, or seek validation in the person they are leading. Instead, they assume that the fact you are there means you want them to guide you, so they lead. There are three ways you can speak intelligently, so anyone instantly views you as an influential leader.

First, you must avoid using slang. Just because your friends understand you does not mean the people you are selling to will. Unless the slang is specific to your industry, known by everyone in your audience, and used tastefully, you should refrain from using it in your sales strategies. Instead, use complete words and sentences that your audience will know and respond to. For example, rather than saying "Sup?" to your audience, say, "How are you?" This way, you come across as engaged, energized, and respectful.

Second, you must avoid mumbling. Enunciating your words in a clear, audible volume ensures everyone hears you and receives your message. This is essential; as people that mishear, you may refrain from purchasing through you because they cannot understand what you are offering. Alternatively, they may purchase through you but misunderstand what you were selling, which could lead to buyers' remorse and a poor experience.

Third, you must avoid using casual language, especially to measure the engagement of your audience. For example, if you teach your client about one of your new products, you should never say "you follow?" or "you know what I mean?" These are casual phrases that make it seem like you are questioning your own knowledge rather than feeling confident. Instead, say, "Do you have any questions?" or "Do you ever experience _____ in your life?" These sound far more intelligent than the former questions and achieve the same outcome.

Say This, Not That

What you say is important, but how you say it is essential. Using the right phrasing ensures that your audience is more likely to positively respond to you, which makes keeping that positive energy far easier. One excellent example of how your language affects your outcome is when someone has been waiting on you as you completed something else. Research has shown that if you say "Sorry for the wait," that person is more likely to have a negative attitude toward you because they are now focused on the wait, rather than the current service. Even if they only waited a short amount of time, it will feel significant to them, and they will behave as though they have been inconvenienced.

On the other hand, if you say, "Thank you for your patience," people positively respond to you. In this case, you have made them feel good about themselves for being patient and have offered positive feedback, making them feel better. They are far more likely to have an excellent attitude with you, now, because you have praised their positive behavior.

Another excellent swap you can make would be, "Are you interested in _____?" for "How can I help you?" If you walk up to someone and they are looking for a particular product, asking if they are interested in that product is partially pointless, and it creates space for them to say "no." Instead, you want to ask, "How can I help you?" because it encourages them to let you know what they are looking for. This approach also keeps you open and receptive, rather than seeming like you are only looking for closed, straight-forward answers.

"Just checking in" is something that should be eliminated from your vocabulary, too. This sounds gimmicky and salesy, and it lacks clarity around what you are checking in on. Instead, ask a direct question that will receive a straightforward answer. For example, you might say, "Hi, have you made any further decisions on _____?" This way, you receive the exact answer you are looking for, which leads you into a more transparent, more productive discussion.

After you have provided someone with information during a sale, it may seem enticing to ask, "Any questions?" however, this is a bad move. If you say this, people will automatically say "no" because they have not had enough time to think about the questions they might have. Instead, you might say, "Are you feeling confident in this?" or "What is most interesting about this to you?" As both of these encourage further discussion.

Lastly, you need to stop saying, "Just wanted to." "Just wanted to check-in." "Just wanted to let you know." "Just wanted to see if you needed any help." "I just wanted to" makes it sound like you are setting someone up to ask them a question or assign them a task, both of which are things people do not want. They will immediately shut down and ignore you because they don't want to "just" do anything. Instead, you should be clear and concise. "I'm checking in because ____." "I am reaching out to let you know ____." "Can I help you with this?" These encourage your recipient to listen and pay attention, rather than shut down and try to get away from the conversation.

Practice Your Sales Language

Practice makes perfect, which is as accurate for mind manipulation as it is for anything else. Regularly practicing your sales language ensures that you develop confidence in your language, as well as in yourself. There are three excellent places to practice language: with the mirror, with your peers, and out in everyday life.

You can practice getting confident with yourself as you say your pitch and make your ask in the mirror. Developing confidence in pitching to yourself makes pitching to other people easier because you overcome a significant portion of your self-confidence concerns. Rather than worrying about how you look, what you are saying, or how someone might judge you, you feel confident because you stand behind how you look, what you are saying, and how you judge yourself.

With your peers, you can practice role-playing different sales circumstances so you can put your skills to use. This is an excellent opportunity to practice making your pitch using appropriate sales language, then receive feedback from the other person. If you practice with people who are also in sales, they can provide you with guidance on how to phrase better your sales language or anything else you can do to improve your results.

In everyday life, you can challenge yourself to random mind manipulation games with other people. For example, you might challenge yourself to get someone to agree to go for coffee with you or give you their number or walk one way rather than another. Creating these challenges allows you to practice your sales language in totally different circumstances and develop confidence in selling anything. When you can confidently manipulate someone's mind to make specific decisions or engage in certain behaviors, you can achieve anything you desire.

CHAPTER 5
Building Strong Rapport

Rapport is a state of harmonious understanding between yourself and another individual or a group. When you achieve a positive connection with someone, you create a sense of trust between them, making manipulation far easier. People who are already skeptical or who have a negative perception of you will refuse to follow along with anything you say because they automatically assume everything you say or do is unhelpful to them. When you have positive rapport, the skepticism is eliminated. People start to believe in you and everything you have to say, which creates that positive association that leads to greater levels of influence.

Building rapport is entirely done through communication and the expression of respect and trust toward the person you are building rapport with. When you can communicate to them in a way that promotes a sense of safety and comfort, and builds trust, people put their guard down and are more accepting toward you and, therefore, your offers.

Break the Ice With New People

One of the most influential moments in any relationship, no matter how small or insignificant that connection may be, is the first impression. An excellent way to build rapport from the first moment you connect with someone is to be willing to break the ice with that person. Rather than waiting for the other person to do it, initiate the conversation yourself in a fun, relaxing way.

As you approach a new person, do so with an open and gentle posture. Keep your shoulders broad, your hips loose, and your hands away from the front of your torso. Ensure you are smiling, and say something warm and friendly to break the verbal ice.

Some excellent sentences to start a conversation with include:
- "Hi, it's a pleasure to meet you! My name is _____, and I'd love to help you with _____ today!"
- "Welcome into _____! What a great day to come in, are you enjoying looking at _____?"
- "Hi, this is Chris with _____. We work with _____ to help them _____. I understand that you are looking for _____?"
- "That's an excellent model of _____! Have you ever used one before?"
- "That's quite the _____ you've got there! Have you had it long?"

Greeting someone with enthusiasm because you are excited to see them or help them is a great way to start a conversation. You can also start one with a genuine compliment on something acceptable for someone in your position to be complimented on. This creates a positive first impression, so the other person is more likely to open up to you and feel confident in your presence.

Use Non-Threatening Language

Jumping directly into personal or pointed conversations can be intimidating to the person you are talking to. When there is something you want from someone else, it can also seem like that is *all* you care about. It is perfectly acceptable to want something from someone and make getting it your objective; however, you should also value making it a positive, fulfilling experience for both of you. That way, you both walk away winners rather than just one of you.

Non-threatening language comprises conversational topics that are non-personal and non-pointed, then gradually moving them toward a more personal and pointed direction. Especially at first, avoid talking about yourself or asking direct questions about the other person. Connect over small things like shared experiences, traveling, the weather, or other candid conversations. Once you begin to share that positive connection and the other person starts sharing more personal information, you can start directing the conversation in a more personal and pointed manner. Although you are directing the conversation, you want to let the other person take the lead. If they seem unwilling to discuss something or private about a particular area of their lives, avoid prying and asking questions. Instead, ask questions about topics they seem more willing to discuss. Following their lead and directing them down the path of least resistance is the best way to get what you desire in a way that feels good for everyone involved.

Listen and Show Empathy

Have you ever spoken to someone that asks questions yet fails to listen or express empathy for your answers? It is awkward and uncomfortable and can build your resentment toward that person. The typical reaction is, "Why ask if you don't care?" Naturally, you do not want to create that experience with a person that you desire to achieve something from, especially since you want them to gain something positive, too.

As you ask questions, or the other person decides to open up, it can help to listen and show empathy for their responses genuinely. Active listening can be achieved by maintaining eye contact, physically facing the other person, and occasionally nodding or agreeing with the other person to show you understand. When the other person is done talking, communicate in a way that shows you understood what they meant, and expresses empathy.

For example, if someone says, "I need a new cell phone because my son broke mine." you might say, "Oh no, your son broke your cell phone? No way! That sucks. Let's get you set up with an excellent replacement." This clarifies that you heard them, expresses empathy, and sets you up to help them discover an excellent solution to their problem.

Leverage Humor Whenever Possible

Laughter has an incredible ability to bring people together and promote bonding, which is why it is so powerful to leverage humor as you establish rapport with people. Whenever possible, inject humor that is appropriate to the situation and the recipient. As you make jokes, focus on joking about yourself or your circumstances, or circumstances that your recipient is likely to find funny as well. Avoid laughing about other people or other people's experiences, as this can make it seem as though you are judgmental and unkind, which can cause people to lack trust in you.

If humor is not your strong suit, it may help to practice simple jokes related to your niche that are sure to make your customers laugh. Having a few pre-canned jokes up your sleeve takes the pressure off as you no longer have to come up with a joke.

Use the Right Non-Verbal Language

Your non-verbal language communicates as much as your verbal language does, if not more. If your spoken language says you are friendly and welcoming, but your non-verbal language says something else, people will be skeptical about you and everything you say. Keep your body language and facial expressions open, light, and relaxed.

Another non-verbal communicator to be aware of is your tone. Speaking in a nervous, tense, or stressed tone will cause people to feel uncomfortable around you as well. Alternatively, if you speak calm and relaxed, you will cause other people to feel more calm and relaxed. A great place to witness the power of this form of communication is with nurses, doctors, or other medical personnel. Most people are already anxious when they go into a medical office, so the people's tone is important. When a nurse speaks to you with a nervous or tense tone, you likely feel more anxious because of how the nurse is talking. When the nurse says calmly and with a reassuring tone, however, you relax because the person you are trusting your wellbeing is relaxed, too. Though you may not be a nurse, you do have the power to manipulate someone to feel more calm and relaxed by keeping your tone as such.

CHAPTER 6
Do The Thinking For Them

What do Nordstrom and prison have in common? They both offer a unique experience. One is positive, and the other is overwhelmingly negative. When you think about shopping in an upscale store like Nordstrom, Simons, Holt Renfrew, or Macy's, you likely think about a well-designed storefront filled with beautiful fashion accessories. When you go, so much thought has been put into your experience that the only thing you have to decide is whether or not you will buy the items you like. If the salesperson has done their job, you will say "yes" more often than not. Why? Because we love having our experiences laid out for us. On the other hand, if someone offered you a stay in jail, you would likely say "no" because we love having *positive* experiences laid out for us.

If you want to get something from someone, you have to do the thinking for them. You must manage the details, consider their needs, and create an experience that they thoroughly enjoy. Saying "yes" to your offer should feel like a natural continuation of the experience because it offers them that sweet ending they're craving. It is like collecting your prize after earning all of the tickets at the amusement park. If you were to leave without claiming your big stuffed dog or inflatable hammer, it would ruin the experience. If you have done everything right, the person you are selling to will want to claim their item in the end, effectively earning you a sale.

Managing someone else's experience and creating a positive opportunity for them to fulfill your request takes thought and effort, yet it is not as challenging as you might think. Once you understand what someone wants and how you can offer it, you create your experience accordingly and invite them into it. From there, the only thing they have to do is say "yes."

You Have the Solution They Need

When someone approaches you for something you are selling, or you come across someone that would be the perfect fit for your product or service, it is essential to remember that you have the solution they need. Regardless of what you are offering, that client needs it in their lives, and you need to keep that in mind so you can show it to them in a way that makes it genuinely enjoyable.

To effectively do the thinking for your recipient regarding the solution they need, you must first intimately understand their concerns and why they are approaching you for an answer. You must empathize with why they need your solution and what, precisely, makes it a selling point for them. For example, let's say you are selling a car to a young couple that just had their first baby. Naturally, they need a vehicle that will fit their growing family, be safe and comfortable, and that won't cost too much as they have recently seen their expenses grow. If you were selling them a vehicle, you would not focus on the horsepower, steering capabilities, or 4 x 4 capabilities of a car. Instead, you would focus on the spaciousness, safety features, and fuel efficiency of the car as these are what they specifically care about.

Tailoring your solution to each individual ensures that you are doing the thinking for them by considering what *they* would think about. When you can speak of an individual's specific concerns, they realize that you are on the same page as they are and can trust your judgment. This is especially true when they know you make decisions similarly to them, and that you empathize with what they need and how they prefer to make decisions. When you establish this point of connection, you do the thinking for them by getting into their minds and telling them how you would do it, which inspires them to behave similarly. Since they now trust you, believe in you, and agree with your choices, they feel confident enough to follow you as their leader, which means you can lead them directly to the decision you want them to make.

The Value of Giving Them Permission

Each of us has a common childhood experience that continues to affect us into adulthood, whether we realize it or not. We are always looking for permission from others to do the things we want to do. As children, we wait for our parents, family, or authority to give us permission to do the things we desire because we know that we might get in trouble if we fail to receive permission. The last thing we want to do is be punished because we were not given explicit permission to make the choice we made. As children, seeking approval is essential because we have not yet learned how to make responsible choices. As we grow up, we may still look to our parents and peers for validation because of this conditioning, and we are extra-sensitive when we feel as though we are not receiving the permission or confirmation we need to make a choice we desire to create.

When people come to you for something, they are also seeking permission to make their desired choice. Even if they are fully grown, years into their independence, or well-established in life, they seek approval. Giving your audience the permission they seek is an excellent way to encourage them to take the action you requested. The thing is, you cannot directly offer approval, nor can you make it seem as though you are telling them what to do. You have to give them implied permission and encourage them to say "yes" to themselves.

Saying something as blatant as "You have my full permission to do this!" no matter how jokingly it may seem, is an excellent way to turn someone off. You come across pushy, demanding, or even condescending when you outright declare that you are giving someone permission. Further, it sounds tacky and even odd. Instead, you need to express that you permit without outright saying it. For example, "You know you want ice cream for dinner tonight, and we won't judge. ;)" or "We have your favorite loafers back in stock! Come get them before they sell out again!" These types of phrases offer permission through a direction of confidence, which results in your audience feeling as though they have received approval to make that choice. For those that were on the fence for reasons they did not understand, this may be all they need to commit to "yes."

Persuading and Leading

There will be many situations where you need to do the thinking for someone else on the fly. You will not always have the opportunity to research each person, case, or offer to ensure that you know how to sell it in the right way. Rather than trying to force the case and saying all the right things, you can practice the art of persuading and leading. This technique enables you to lead the conversation subliminally so that you can learn as you go, allowing you to make up your pitch and sell on the spot.

To persuade someone, you want to focus on asking them questions about the specific offer you have. Do not start out asking about the proposal itself. Instead, ask questions that will help you better understand how and why the proposal would suit that person's needs. For example, if you are selling a new software for their computer, ask them how they use their computer and what types of experiences they enjoy most when browsing the internet. Build insight into what they are looking for, then offer them some direction. Once they take it, build further insight into what they need, then provide more guidance. Continue persuading and leading the conversation in this way until you reach the point where you are ready to make your offer.

CHAPTER 7
Use The Snowball Effect

If you are looking for a superhero card that you can pull from your back pocket and close more deals, you need to use the snowball effect. This tactic encourages people to get in a positive frame of mind, teaches them to say "yes," opens them up to your opportunity, and sets them up for a "yes." What's more, is this strategy is straightforward to incorporate into your sales strategy and will drastically improve your results.

Getting the Initial "Yes"

The snowball effect requires you to do everything you can to get people to say "yes." You want them to agree with everything you say, which means you need to say nice things. As you get your recipient used to saying yes, avoid worrying too much about what they are saying yes to, as you can direct their attention later.

For now, you can ask questions like:
- "Are you enjoying this weather?"
- "Have you been enjoying your weekend?"
- "Are you looking forward to summer break?"
- "Do you enjoy using _____?"
- "Have you used _____ before?"

An easy way to get people to say yes is to ask questions that involve information that has already been told to you, so you know someone is going to say "yes." For example, if someone says, "I am still not sure what computer I should buy!" You could say, "Have you been looking for a while?" which they will more than likely say yes to since they have already hinted this to be true. Paying attention to cues and clues is a great way to connect deeper with your client while also knowing what questions will get you a "yes" response.

Once you have received a handful of positive responses to your questions, you can focus on directing questions toward your sale. At this point, your recipient is feeling positive and is having a good experience with you, so they are ready to have a good experience during a sale, too.

Accelerating Your "Yes"

Following some basic "yes" answers, you are ready to begin accelerating your way through the conversation. In other words, you need to continue asking questions that will fetch you positive responses, but you need to start asking more significant questions. Since you are focused on selling something, you want to ask questions to direct the conversation toward that sale. You need to do it in a way that still comes across as compassionate, empathetic, respectful, and fun. If you overthink this part, your tone will change, and you will begin stumbling over your words, so you need to keep this as light-hearted and comfortable as the rest of the sale.

Once you have moved through the basic questions, an excellent way to begin accelerating your "yeses" is to make safe assumptions regarding your client's needs so you can draw them toward your solution. Your safe assumptions need to be ones that you confidently believe to be true about your customer based on clues and cues they have given you. For example, if you are talking to a mom with a young child, you can safely assume that their child is spirited, their schedule is busy, or they are in serious need of some personal time. Present these safe assumptions as a question, and use them to draw your customer toward the sale. With the mom, you might say, "You must be super busy?" and she would say, "Yes." Then you might say, "Would you value a product that could give you back some of your free time?" and she would likely say "Yes" again. From there, you can show her a few highlights of that product and ask if she wants to learn more. If she does, you go ahead and make the pitch then offer the sale.

The challenging part about the accelerating yes is that you have to ask at a reasonable pace to the customer, and you have to ask in a way that sets you up for the sale. It helps to zoom out and focus on the more significant picture and continually work toward understanding why your product or service suits their bigger picture needs. As you do, ask questions that gear your client in the same direction so they, too, see how your product or service is an excellent fit for them.

Getting a "Yes" On the Sale

If you have already been enjoying a lively conversation filled with positive feedback, getting to a "yes" on your sale will be effortless. You have effectively crafted an enjoyable experience, and your client wants to go home with their "prize." However, you must ask at the right time, and in the right way, if you will get the yes, you desire. Essentially, the ask must be a natural extension of the existing conversation so that they continue to remain in that positive flow. If you change your tone, adjust your approach, or shift gears now, you will break the flow, and your client may find themselves second-guessing everything. Remember, this isn't about manipulating someone into something they do not need. It is about driving someone into realizing that what they already desire is available to them and that now is the right time to say "yes." You are serving for the good of all, and you must maintain that perspective as you go in for the big ask. Determining when to ask for the sale can be achieved by recognizing the nonverbal and verbal clues that indicate a person is ready for the offer.

Nonverbal cues can be read through eye contact, expressions, and body language. If you notice someone feeling relaxed, making eye contact, and listening to what you have to say without feeling tense, stressed, or disinterested, you have come across someone ready to receive the pitch. If their eyes are darting around, they avoid eye contact, or they seem stressed or checked out, it is not time to make your ask. Physically, a person with their posture open, relaxed, and welcoming is more willing to be pitched to. However, if they have their hands crossed, they are closed off, trying to leave, or seem fully turned away from you, which indicates they are not ready for the sale. Lastly, you want to look for visual cues of readiness. Smiling, nodding, and leaning in toward you are excellent signs of enthusiasm. You can also look for the tone of voice and volume to identify whether someone is ready for the sale.

Verbally, if someone is ready for the sale, they will be pushing for you to give them more information. Someone that actively asks questions and listens to the answers and invites further information is ready to say "yes." The more someone asks you for information, requests to see evidence, and presses for knowledge, the closer they are to saying "yes." Your entire focus should be on answering these questions and giving them the direction they need so they can get their way to "yes." If you set the conversation up correctly, you may not even have to ask because *they* will be asking *you* for the sale, which means *you* will be the one saying "yes!"

CHAPTER 8
Receive An Inch, Take A Mile

In this day and age, everyone is used to being sold to and is well aware of an impending sales conversation when they see one coming. Whether they are approaching you for the sale, or you are approaching them, they know they are about to find themselves in a conversation. Because of this, people have also mastered their unique way of politely exiting the sales conversation before anything comes of it. Primarily because they do not want to waste their time or endure an uncomfortable pitch when they inevitably say "no." This means that if someone does not immediately exit a conversation and instead shows interest in what you have to say, you should take that interest and run with it. A person that is willing to give you attention without immediately rejecting the conversation is a person that is interested in what you have to offer. If you use that moment wisely, you will have their ear long enough to make the sale. If, however, you do not immediately take advantage of that moment to increase their interest, they will grow bored and end the conversation.

Anytime you are selling something, you must always position yourself as the leader and control any conversation you enter. While you want to emphasize your client's focus and make them the star of the conversation, it is up to you to make them the star and use that to motivate them in your desired direction.

People Want Direction

People are abundantly terrified of making the wrong decisions. Especially when it comes to purchasing something or engaging with something they are unfamiliar with, they are afraid of doing it wrong and suffering unknown consequences as a result. That is why they love salespeople: the right salesperson will recognize their need, provide them with adequate knowledge, and support them with making the right choice. If they take the time to trust and follow the right person, they will have an excellent experience without any unwanted consequences.

Realizing that people want direction, no matter how significant or insignificant your offer may be, allows you to own your position as the honorary director. In other words, you are the one that has the knowledge they need to make the choices they want, so now you must assume the role and direct them to make the right choices. They rely on you to know exactly what they want and need and direct them to make a choice they will be satisfied with, and if you do this well, they will look back on the experience happily. They will even send more people your way and offer you more opportunities to direct others through the same process, effectively increasing your ability to close more deals.

When someone has come to you and asked a question or shown interest in your offer, you must assume that they want your direction and act accordingly. Your number one focus should be to accept your role of offering guidance, building rapport, and offering advice based on what you learn. When you create a sense of direction that precisely fits the person you are directing, you achieve far greater success in your role, and mind manipulation becomes effortless. This way, you are working with their natural state to bring it in your desired direction, rather than pushing against it or attempting to force them in an order unnatural to who they are.

Offering Casual Direction

Casual directions are an excellent way to begin the process of stepping into the leadership role when someone approaches you. This is the very first step you should take, as it allows people to become used to seeing you as their leader, so they warm up to the idea of following what you tell them to do. Casual directions rarely have anything to do with your offer. Instead, they are more focused on conditioning that person to follow your instruction. These directions can start immediately upon meeting a new person, as this is the best time to offer the first impression of being a safe, trustworthy leader they can follow.

The first direction you give someone should invite them into your space or into a conversation with you. You might say, "That's a really cool _____. Have you seen _____ before?" and if they say "No," you say, "Come with me, I'll show you! You're going to love it." Or, you might say, "I love that! Have you heard of it before?" and if they say "No," you say, "Let me tell you a bit about it!"

Offering these types of directions right from the start shows that you are enthusiastic, excited to guide them through a positive experience, and willing to make that experience worth their while. You should continue offering casual direction and continually increase your position as an authority figure in the conversation.

Some excellent casual direction you might offer would be:
- "Why don't you sit down so we can talk?"
- "Stand here, and I'll show you _____."
- "Send me a message so we can discuss _____."
- "Show me your existing _____."
- "Tell me about your experience with _____."
- "Let me take that for you."
- "Put your email here, and I'll send you more information."
- "Give me the details."
- "Come with me, and I'll show you _____."
- "Save my number in your phone, so you can call me _____ to discuss _____."

These directions focus on guiding someone through an experience, without directing them straight to the sale. There is nothing wrong with taking your time and warming someone up, while priming their mind, to create the results you desire. As you begin this sense of direction and continue to connect with the individual, you build rapport and make them feel more trusting in you, closing the sale far easier.

Directing Them to "Yes"

When the individual you are talking to is saying "yes" to everything, following your directions, and appearing enthusiastic and engaged in the conversation, you are ready to direct them to "yes." This is where you have to be careful, though, as you do not want to appear as though you are bossing them into a sale or forcing them to make a decision that they might not be ready to make yet. Rather than leading with a direction, you would be better to lead with a question and end with an order.

The question allows you to decide whether they are ready for the sale or not yet. To avoid receiving a "No," it is better to ask a question with two finite answers, as this allows you to direct them on a solution that is more favorable to your results. For example, rather than saying "Are you ready to purchase ____?" or "So, do you want to purchase ____?" which could lead to a "No," you would say, "You've learned a lot of great information today, would you like to walk away with your new ____, or do you need more time to think it over?" This way, if they *do* have a "No" response in mind, you shift it toward a less closed response, as they decide they want to think it over. The direction you offer following this question depends on what the person answers.

If they answer yes, you direct them through the rest of the sale. This is where you gather their desired items, ring them through, and close the deal. It is essential that throughout the entire process, and even after the close, you continue to maintain a charismatic, charming personality, as you do not want them to feel as though they made a mistake. Their experience matters from start to finish, including any follow-up questions they might have after the sale. If you take the mile to offer an excellent experience from top to bottom, you will be far more likely to generate the results you want and the results you need.

If they choose to wait, you need to direct them on how long to wait and how to proceed once they decide. You should never leave this as an open-ended follow-up, as this makes it challenging for either of you to know when to follow up with the other.

Instead, you want to say something like:
- "I totally get it; this is a big decision to make! Why don't you take my number and give me a call on Tuesday so I can answer any questions you think about over the next few days?"

- "I like to ask my (wife/husband) before making big choices, too. I'll be back by Saturday. Why don't you bring them down, and we can all discuss this together?"
- "This is a lot to process. Let me give you a pamphlet that covers everything we discussed today so you can look it over, and I can call you on Thursday to see if you have any questions."

These directions encourage them to continue thinking about the decision and follow up with you or receive your follow up later so you can continue the conversation. If you give someone a direction to follow up and they agree, but then fail to follow up, you can always follow up a day or two after the proposed follow-up date to ask them how they are doing. In this case, you would say, "Hey ____! I didn't hear from you on ____, so I wanted to call you about ____ to see if I could answer any questions you might have!" This way, your follow up is welcomed and well-received, rather than seen as random or pushy.

CHAPTER 9
Your Real Deadline Is Not Your Declared Deadline

In sales, your real deadline should never be your declared deadline. Regardless of how passionate a salesperson you are or how excellent you are with closing, you still need to rely on someone else to make an agreeable decision to close t1eehe sale. If you offer the genuine deadline as your deadline, then the opportunity ends when the deadline passes. Unfortunately, many people will decide to say "yes" too late. Essentially, they realize *after* that they wish they would have said yes, but they were unaware of their desire until they realized it was no longer an option. Recognizing this and using this knowledge to your advantage is an excellent way to use deadlines to your advantage so you can close more sales. Plus, you end up closing those sales well before the real deadline passes.

Deadline-Motivated Obligations

Whenever you want to manipulate someone to make a decision, you have to give them a deadline. Proposed decisions without deadlines are never made because the person responsible for making the decision feels as though they have limitless time to make that decision. This is why massive corporations release limited-edition products or time-sensitive sales because they want people to hurry up and decide already. Their time-sensitive offers always sell better than anything else because people are afraid of missing out or wishing they had made a choice sooner. With products or offers with no limitations or deadlines, the person can "think it over" indefinitely, because the opportunity to act is not going anywhere.

You can offer deadline-motivated obligations in many ways, ranging from a deadline to purchase to a deadline to follow up with you. These deadlines will linger in a person's mind and motivate them to pay attention, so they are more likely to decide or take follow-up action.

To propose a deadline motivated obligation, you want to indicate a pressing deadline, without making yourself sound pushy. Saying something intrusive like "You should decide today because the sale is ending!" or "Follow up with me by tomorrow. Otherwise, someone else might buy it!" will damage your selling abilities because people begin to think you are trying to force them, rather than leave them to make their own choices. You need to trust your client to make their own choices, but give them the tools they need to make the choices you want them to make. You can do this by saying things like:
- "Totally, think it over! I will let you know that this sale ends _____, though. Here's my number if you want to take advantage of this deal before it ends!"

- "Take your time! Let's touch base again Friday, so I can set you up before the sale ends if you decide to go for it!"
- "It's definitely worth thinking about. This deal ends Saturday, so message me at this number _____ by then if you decide you are ready to buy."
- "I won't be in again until Monday, but you can come to see if it is still here on that day if you decide you want it."

These sentences motivate people to take action because they realize there is only so much time for that action to be taken. In many cases, a definite deadline is all a person needs to come back and make a choice to purchase.

Just-Before-the-Deadline Sale

Once you have offered a deadline, you must know that the average person will not come back until right before that deadline passes. This is because, at first, they have plenty of time to decide, so they take their time. They often mull over the decision, imagine living without it, and figure out that there is still plenty of time left if they decide to change their minds.

Come to the deadline, though, they begin to realize how much they want what you have to offer. Suddenly, the client knows it will no longer be available, so they reconsider. Now, they are eager to come in and make a deal. After all, they can't imagine passing up the offer and missing out on something the client truly wanted or having to pay more for it because they waited too long.

When a person comes back before the deadline, it is important to celebrate them and reward them with an excellent experience. Cheer them on, show enthusiasm through their purchase, and enjoy the process with them. The more you do this, the better they feel about their choice, and the more likely they are to refer you to other people. Because of how enthusiastic their referrals are, based on their positive experience, they will already have their friends and family excited to have the same excellent experience, which means your referral-based sales will be even more accessible.

The Past-the-Deadline Sale

Some people have to wait for the deadline to pass entirely before they realize they actually wanted something. As soon as it is no longer available, they realize they are missing out, and they scramble to try to get a hold of the lost opportunity. This is where proposed deadlines matter: if you offered a proposed deadline that was different from the real deadline, you gain the opportunity to honor the offer and make the sale. The key here is that you cannot lie about the real deadline. For example, if your company is advertising that there is a sale until Friday and you say the sale ends Wednesday, your client knows you are lying and will not trust you or buy from you. If, however, you say the sale ends Friday, but you won't be in again after Wednesday, you are not lying, and you have offered a specific deadline prior to the real deadline. This way, if Wednesday passes and they realize they did, in fact, want to make a purchase, you can come in or take over a shift before Friday so you can close the sale.

After a deadline has passed, it is important that you make the urgency clear. You may also play the role of the hero, as you "ask your boss" if you can extend the deadline for that client, or you hold a "special space" for them to take advantage of the deal, even though it has already technically ended. Or, perhaps you say nothing but express your relief that the desired item was still available when they came in. Either way, you want to play into the idea that they are lucky that the deal still exists, as this encourages them to feel good about making the decision and motivates them to see it all the way through. Never punish someone for waiting until after the proposed deadline, because in doing so, you may make them feel bad. Instead, celebrate them and show enthusiasm just as you would with anyone else.

CHAPTER 10
Give More Than You Take

There is a phenomenon in the human condition that leads to people feeling a sense of obligation to those that do something kind for them. Every one of us experiences it, and it massively affects the way we interact with others'. If you want to have the upper hand when it comes to mind manipulation, you can take advantage of this by always giving more than you take. When you express generosity at every opportunity you have, people feel obligated to return the gesture, which can be used to your benefit in many ways.

Specifically, in sales, being generous means that once you reach the point of making your pitch, the person you have pitched to feels a sense of obligation to say "yes." While you are not forcing them to say yes, their inner need to keep things balanced or stay out of debt to another person has them wanting to agree to whatever you ask of them. This is where you can close sales effortlessly, solely based on how you show up to the other person's experience.

This act of giving and receiving is one that often feels unnatural to people, as placing your entire emphasis on the other person may take away from you getting what you desire. However, if you look at it from a bigger-picture perspective, you realize that if you give more than you take, then what you receive has the ability to contain far more value to you. For example, in a sale, it is inevitable that you have to give some of your time toward making the sale, so if you take the extra effort to make that a wonderful experience, it doesn't take much out of you. When you reach the end of the sale, how much you gave directly affects what you receive in return, though. If you did not give adequately, you are unlikely to receive anything significant, which may make it seem as though you wasted your energy. If, however, you gave abundantly, you are far more likely to receive a sale, which means you gain something valuable for minimal output. As you get habituated to creating this experience for others, it becomes easier for you to make generous offers and receive abundantly in return.

It's About the Experience You Give

When I say "give more than you take," I do not mean that you need to physically give the other person something. As you conduct your sales call, for example, you do not have to offer to give up your coat, your car, or a bunch of money to have the other person wanting to give back to you. If this were the case, the give-and-take concept would be terrible, as you would end up with nothing left by the end of your sales call.

Though physically giving someone something is valuable, it is less about *what* you give and more about *how* you give it. Your entire focus should be on providing the other person with a wonderful experience that stimulates them to feel good. If they feel happy, curious, excited, interested, inspired, fulfilled, or any other sort of positive emotion, you have created a wonderful experience for that person. This means when it comes time for you to ask for a favor or a sale, they feel obligated to say yes. Moreover, they feel good about saying yes because you have given them so much that they are happy to oblige. This means you not only make the sale or get your needs fulfilled; you also get positive reviews, which can lead to referrals and more opportunities.

The experience you give should cover three focal points: the emotions, the story, and the gift. Fulfilling all three elements of the experience will ensure that you spread enough generosity that the other person wants to give back to you, too.

The emotions of the experience are simple: you want the other person to feel *good*. In days gone by, much of sales was oriented around stimulating fear in someone, then providing them a solution to their fear. This often worked because fear is a wonderful motivator, and if you promise to eliminate someone's fear, then you are the "hero." These days, most people can see right through that behavior, so they are unlikely to fall for it. In fact, they may even be annoyed that you used it or try to steer clear of your business to avoid feeling bad in the future. Instead, you want to stimulate positive feelings through your experience.

While the feelings are the objective, the story is the experience itself. You want to walk people through a specific story or experience from start to finish. For example, consider most luxury fashion shops. Their "story" is that you need to be pampered, and you want to be pampered while you invest in yourself. As you walk through the door, you are often greeted with a smiling face, a personal shopper, and a glass of champagne. You are escorted through the store, then brought to a private shopping area where you can sit, relax, and enjoy being pampered by your shopper. Likely, they behave as though you are long-time friends because they know you are looking for a friendly experience where you feel as though you are "hanging out with the girls" or "hanging out with the guys." They will bring a mirror and help you dress into many different outfits and lavish you with compliments as you get dressed. Eventually, you purchase your items and leave, after having a wonderful experience in-store. Do you get the point? There should always be a start, middle, and finish. The start should be the welcome or the invitation that encourages someone to come talk to you, the middle should be the part where you spoil them and get to know them, and the finish should be where they make their purchase. The finish should be the least-emphasized part of the process, as you worry more about their experience through the start and middle.

Lastly, you want to focus on the gift. Physically giving someone something is a wonderful way to cement in your generosity and make them feel as though they need to give you something in return... like their money! In luxury stores, employees often give people a glass of champagne, a comfortable place to sit, and a few snacks to enjoy while they shop. Some stores give away catalogs, free swag, or coupons. In a sales setting, you could even give someone your business card and your number so they can contact you with any needs they might have. If you are using mind manipulation in a private setting, there is no limit on what you can give someone to illicit their inner need of giving back. You may give them flowers, gum, a drink, a small present, or even a meal from a restaurant. Get creative and offer something relevant to them, and what you want from them, so they feel obligated to give back in the same general way. This way, you are far more likely to get what you want and need out of someone.

The Giving Is in the Details

If you want to stand apart from the average person that will be using the "give and take" tactic to earn sales or anything else they desire, you must focus on the details. The details are where you get to take someone from having a good experience, to having a phenomenal experience, which makes you far more memorable. While you do want to refine your approach and get as specific as possible, you do not want to waste time creating your detailed approach. Instead, you can use someone else's approach to define how you will approach yours, which is an extremely easy way to rapidly one-up the competition and earn your desired results. To create the details, you will start by identifying three different experiences: two you like from your niche, and one you like from outside your niche. You may also want to identify an experience you do not like, so you can scan your own experience to avoid adding those unwanted elements to it.

You want to carefully analyze each of the three or four experiences to see what you like most about them, and how you can implement them into your own experience. Then, you will define your *basic* experience. That's right. The experience you define based on everyone else's will be your basic experience. To one-up the competition, you have to go above and beyond. To do this, you will identify where your basic experience can be improved or can become even more thoughtful. This is where looking to experiences outside of your niche can be helpful, as they allow you to bring in a unique perspective and approach. Once you have defined 2-3 details, you will add that go above and beyond the competition. You can practice running through the experience you will be offering.

It is important that you continually look to the details to offer even more assistance, as frequently as possible. You do not want to drastically transform your experience time and again, but you do want to expand on it so that it evolves over time and becomes even more enjoyable for your clients. This is an excellent way to stay relevant, while also offering fresh experiences for repeat clients. In this way, you offer the same service they know and love, with added bonuses each time they return.

The final way you will adjust your details is by listening carefully to the feedback you receive. Anytime you bring someone through the experience, listen to what they say about you and the way you helped them, and use that to refine your experience even further. If they have negative comments or complaints, you can adjust your approach to ensure you are strengthening your weaknesses and offering a genuinely enjoyable experience. If they have positive comments or compliments, use that to reinforce those parts of your service, or to add that extra element to other areas of your service. This is another way that you can give-and-take with your clients, where they give you feedback, and you take it to make a better experience so you can earn more sales over time.

Go Out of Your Way to Be Helpful

Anytime you want to get something from someone, be it a sale or their agreement on something, it can be easy to get caught up in *your* experience. You become so fixated on your results that you lose sight of what needs to happen in order for those results to be achieved. If you spend the entire time focused on yourself and what you intend on getting out of a deal, you lose sight of the fact that if the other person doesn't agree, *you aren't getting those results.*

While you may feel fixated on yourself and your own achievements, it is important to make the entire experience about *them*. Focus all of your energy and attention on the person you are selling to or using manipulation tactics on, so they feel like they are the star of the show. Complement them, give them as much help as you can, make their life easier, and generally be a light in their life. Anytime they communicate with you – before, during, or after the sale – they should feel as though you are genuinely committed to making life better for them.

The essential factor here is that you do not fixate solely on being generous around what you want to receive from them. Be generous in as many ways as you can. If you are helping a couple purchase a trailer and they comment that they want it because they intend on driving to visit their children in a different state, give them a few tips on what they should do when they are in that state. Or, give them guidance on how they can make their travel easier, cost-effective, or more enjoyable.

Don't stop there. Go completely out of your way to help them, if you need to. For example, let's say you are in the middle of a sale, and your client mentions they are hungry and have yet to stop for lunch. Stop, recommend a place they eat, and even offer to help them set up a reservation if it is a restaurant that takes reservations. Offering help that is above and beyond what they came to you for shows that you are committed to serving them and makes them feel as though you are genuinely there to make their life better and easier. When they realize how kind and caring you are, they will trust you more, and they will be far more likely to purchase through you, too. Even if they don't purchase that day, you will be the person they come back to see because they want to support you the same way you supported them.

Follow Through on Your Agreements

Following through is the golden standard in sales, and it counts for *everything*. Follow through when it comes to arranging a sale, completing a sale, and even after a sale. If you say you will do something, no matter what it is, do it. If you cannot do it, don't say you will. Sticking to your word is essential, as it teaches people they can trust you and encourages them to feel loyal to you, too.

During the sales process, if you promise to teach your client about their new product or show them something, make sure it happens. If it doesn't, write it down and follow up with them as soon as you can to offer to fulfill that promise. Invite people to come back and ask you for help anytime they need, and if they return, help them. Even if they are not making any further purchases, fulfill their need for assistance, and they will give back to you, too. The positive feedback, reviews, and referrals you gain from this type of giving behavior will always pay itself back over time.

Another way you can give to your clients is to give them the expectation of you following up. Anytime you conduct a sales call, sell something, or otherwise interact with a client, always set the expectation that you will follow up at a specific time. This way, they expect a follow-up, and they do not feel annoyed or pressured when they receive it. Instead, they see that you are following through on your promise, which builds rapport and trust.

CHAPTER 11
Stand For Something Big

What you stand for makes all the difference when it comes to generating success with your goals. This approach has been used for decades by people of all walks of life as a way to motivate themselves to work consistently toward achieving their goals. When you stand for something bigger than yourself, it becomes easier to push yourself. In life, we sadly become all too willing to let ourselves down, disappoint ourselves, and even hurt ourselves if we think the immediate gratification of the alternative is worth it. Using yourself as your motivator is unlikely to be strong enough, so it helps to make your purpose about more than just you.

In sports, people often motivate themselves by attaching their drive to a specific person. Major sports stars will use their children, partners, siblings, parents, grandparents, friends, even their idols as motivation to do better. They want to win, not just for themselves, but for that person they are in it for. In their minds, if they fail, they let that person down, so they *must* win. While they might be able to convince themselves that letting themselves down is not the worst thing, they simply cannot convince themselves that letting their special person down would be okay. So, they don't. They show up, train hard, play hard, and win as many achievements as they can to honor that person they are showing up for. Take a page from their script and stand for something bigger than yourself if you want to drive yourself to win.

Figure Out Which Emotion Drives You

Humans are generally driven by one of two things: pain or pleasure. If you are driven by pain, you are driven to avoid pain. If you are driven by pleasure, you are driven to pursue pleasure. Most of us are driven to avoid pain, based on the biological makeup of our brains, which are wired with what psychologists call "negativity bias." This bias means we are likely to see the worst in everything for the sole purpose of it driving us to avoid those negatives so we can keep ourselves safe. Every human has it, though we all experience it to varying degrees.

Your first step to finding something bigger than yourself to stand for is identifying whether you are driven to avoid pain or pursue pleasure. Once you know which drives you most, you can start identifying specific emotions that you want to avoid or pursue. Ideally, you should get specific and identify the most painful or pleasurable emotion that you want to avoid or pursue. The more it drives your emotional response, the more likely you will be to take that motivator seriously and use it to your advantage.

The emotional attachment here is essential, as it will drive you to do everything it takes to get the results you desire. When your emotional driving force is bigger than yourself, you become motivated to get confident, stay persistent, and do whatever it takes to see your outcome through. Many people will not factor in an emotional driving force, which results in them being demotivated by the simplest obstacles, thus preventing them from achieving their desires.

Pick a Person That Stimulates That Emotion

Each one of us has a person in our lives that can stimulate the emotion you need to help you get through any obstacle you are up against. This person can stimulate you positively or negatively. For example, your daughter might motivate you to become a better person, so you work hard to avoid disappointing her. Alternatively, your dad may have been an awful guy, so you work hard to prove him wrong about who you really are. It does not matter how the person motivates you, as long as they motivate you strongly enough that you feel an immediate rush of the need to get into action.

You might feel motivated to pick a few people that emotionally drive you, especially if you have many that trigger strong emotional responses from within. While you can certainly have as many as you desire, I suggest you focus on just one as too many could become chaotic and overwhelming. Pick the person that *most* drives you, and use that as the primary person that drives you to achieve your results.

If you find that you feel driven but have not yet reached the point of "have to," you may need to have a mental discussion with the person you have chosen. Or, if the circumstances call for it, you can commit to that person directly and let them know that you are pursuing excellence because of them. Having a conversation with that person, whether it be mental or real, gives you the opportunity to commit to them and clarify why you are committing to them in the first place. This solidifies your reasoning and reinforces your commitment to that person, which can take your emotional drive and make it that much stronger.

Attach Yourself to Fulfilling Your Bigger Purpose

Once you have committed to your bigger purpose or the person that is driving you to achieve success, you must take your commitment seriously. Commitment is not driven by saying something, but by following through on what you have said, and that is driven by decision. You must continually decide to remain committed to that person, see through your commitment, and go the extra mile. Ideally, your commitment to that person should elicit a strong enough emotion that makes you *want* to see your commitment through every time you are faced with a relevant decision.

The benefit of this is, you can use that person and the emotions they invoke to drive you to do anything. You can run the furthest, score the most goals, make the most sales, recruit the most people, or create the best possible outcome in whatever you desire, all based on how you want to fulfill your commitment to that person. Since it is your commitment to them, and likely not something they asked of you, you get to decide how that looks and what you will do to fulfill it.

Anytime you are in a position where you need to fulfill your commitment, think about that person, invoke those emotions, and make it happen. Before you go into a significant meeting with your boss, think about your mom and how you promised you would make her proud and how you want to avoid making her disappointed. As you enter a new sale, think about your son and how you promised you would show him anything is possible, and you want to avoid making him feel otherwise. Invoke those thoughts and feelings, and use them to drive your confidence, determination, and strategy. You are far more likely to show up as a convincing, persuasive, authoritative individual if you approach every situation this way.

CHAPTER 12
Be Shameless

The negative associations with manipulation cause many people to believe that mind manipulation is something that you should be guilty, embarrassed, or even ashamed of. This mindset is driven by people assuming that, in order to get what you want, you have to take something away from another person. Of course, this may be true for a few people out there, but it is not true of everyone. In fact, most people that are using manipulation tactics to get what they want are genuinely pursuing something that would make their lives better, while also making the other person's life better. Or, at the very least, it is something that is natural and reasonable for them to expect of the other person, and manipulation is merely used as a way to ensure they get it.

If you get worked up and feel like you do not deserve to get what you want, or you feel ashamed for trying to get what you want, you must dig into the core of what is causing this. Knowing why you feel ashamed for having wants or needs, and wishing for them to be fulfilled, allows you to heal this issue so you can pursue your desires shamelessly.

The Perspective You Have

A perspective many have is that by wanting or needing something, they are inconveniencing or even harming another person. While this is untrue, it is a common belief people have. Usually, this is rooted in childhood experience where you had a want or a need and were made to feel like it was entirely unreasonable for you to have it.

You might have heard things like:
- "I don't have time for that."
- "We can't afford that."
- "I can buy groceries, or your toy, which will it be?"
- "If I play with you, then I can't work."
- "I don't have time for you. I have to do _____."
- "I can't buy you that. I need that money for _____."
- "But if you keep playing with that toy you like, then Jimmy doesn't get a turn. That isn't fair."

These types of sentiments are seemingly harmless, but they instill within us this belief that by wanting something, we are doing something wrong or asking too much of someone else. This is entirely untrue. Wants and needs are natural and normal, and we all have them. Recognizing and desiring to fulfill your wants and needs is neither selfish nor wrong. There may be wrong ways to fulfill your wants or needs, but there are also plenty of positive, meaningful ways to fulfill them.

If you find yourself feeling guilty or ashamed of asking someone for something, such as the sale, you are unlikely to show up with conviction. Rather than being confident, committed, and thorough, you will lack confidence, commitment, and attention to detail. Likely, you will make all the mistakes that mess up your sale, rather than all the decisions that help you see it through. Feelings of shame, especially when they are caused because we think we are hurting someone, are difficult to deal with. Fortunately, it doesn't have to be that way. And, if you were to zoom out and honestly assess the situation, you would realize it was never that way to begin with.

The Perspective You Need

The perspective you need to keep in mind is that your motivating factor is *not* about harming another individual. The very fact that you are so worried about it to the point of feeling ashamed means that this is the opposite of what you want to do. What you actually want to do is have your wants or needs fulfilled while also helping the other person feel positive around the role they play in the experience. In other words, you want to see a win-win situation.

Wants and needs are inherent; wanting to hurt or bug someone is not. No matter what you do, you will never relieve yourself of having wants or needs, though you can (easily) find ways to get those desires fulfilled without harming anyone in the process. There are countless ways that you can approach a situation to encourage a double-positive, as long as you are willing to put in the effort to do so.

The first step to cleaning up your perspective is to own that you want to create a positive experience for everyone involved. In the best-case scenario, you would both walk away with a want or need fulfilled, which is what you are actively working toward. Then, you can intentionally discard any manipulative behaviors that would cause you to get your way without the other person having their wants or needs met. For example, sleazy sales tactics that profit on confusion and mysticism, rather than honesty and a genuine desire to fulfill.

Lastly, you need to adjust your perspective around the outcome, too. If your approach is to ensure that you both win, you need to accept it if the other person says there is no chance for them to win in that situation. If you are selling something they don't want or need, for example, it is okay for them to admit that and decide not to purchase it. You can still have your needs met by having that person refer other, more suitable people to you. Or, you can focus on the fact that there are still plenty of people you can connect with to make your offer to. Not everyone is going to want what you have to offer, but your need is not to sell to every single person. Your need is to sell *enough,* and you need to feel confident that enough people want what you have and will absolutely experience the win-win you are offering.

Five Steps to Shameless

Shifting your perspective is an excellent way to begin to shift your feelings, though there is still plenty you can do to uproot those feelings of shame and encourage yourself to feel shameless in sales. These tactics are not meant to pave the way for you to engage in a darker manipulation strategy; rather, they are to help you feel more confident in using your positive strategies to encourage your desired outcome. In other words, these will help you feel better about asking for your wants and needs to be met under any circumstances, whether it is directly related to sales or not!

Creating a sense of shamelessness starts with identifying what you want, committing to it, and knowing within the depths of yourself that it is possible for you to achieve this. In sales, you must know that you want to close a sale and commit to seeing it through. When you know at the bottom of your very existence what you want and that you deserve to make it happen, it becomes far easier for you to maintain shamelessness around your desires.

Each one of us has a sense of authority ingrained within us. We have the capacity to turn away from any sense of negativity, criticism, or feelings of unnecessary guilt by embracing our inner authority, giving ourselves permission to see things through, and then doing it. Just like your mom would have told you to get your room clean as a kid, and you would have seen it through, do the same as an adult. Your mom had no shame asking you to follow through, nor should you.

Follow-through is, and always will be, the most important thing you can do. If you want to develop a sense of shamelessness, you have to actually make it happen. Go out and behave shamelessly, even if it feels totally uncomfortable at first. Fake it for as long as you have to until you can genuinely embrace shamelessness.

Practicing is, by far, one of the most important things you can possibly do. The first time you go out and attempt to rock your shamelessness, you will not feel entirely shameless. You are going to feel levels of shame, even though they may be lower than what you are used to. Or, maybe they feel the same, but you go anyway because you are ready to follow through and make a change. If you stop there, however, you will never reach the point of true shamelessness. You must continue to practice this approach until it feels good, and then carry on after that, too.

Lastly, you need to say empowering things to yourself. All too often, after we finish something meaningful, we beat ourselves up, rather than build ourselves up. If you are fixated on what you should have done, or how you should have approached the situation, rather than what you did do, you are not helping yourself. Constructive criticism is always welcome, but bullying yourself for not doing better, or for coming across a certain way, is never helpful. Instead, when you reflect on how you have behaved, reflect lovingly and with the intention of boosting yourself, rather than holding yourself back. Through this, you find your way into self-induced shamelessness.

CHAPTER 13
The Power Of Body Language

Body language is a powerful form of communication that connects with others in deep conscious and subconscious ways. Unless someone is intentionally reading another person's body language for cues, this language is often subconscious, which means it reaches your audience in a non-obvious manner. Body language serves as an excellent way to manipulate the minds of others, as it enables you to speak to the part of their brain that decides whether they feel good or bad about something. In the subconscious mind, each of us automatically judges situations, people, and other factors as being good or bad. Naturally, if you want to get something from someone, you want them to judge you as being good, trustworthy, and genuine. You can achieve this by communicating with them in a primal way, through body language.

The body language you use to communicate with others will vary between different circumstances; however, the general flow of things will always be the same. In sales, you want to use body language that has you coming off as a casual, authoritative individual that is trustworthy and service-oriented. This way, you create a warm, welcoming environment that allows the other person to feel secure in going through you to fulfill their needs, which means you also fulfill your own needs.

Another benefit of body language is that you can use body language to identify how your client is feeling and what you can do to improve your odds of getting what you need from them. When you are able to adequately read the cues they give you, it becomes effortless to determine what the best course of action is to get them to do what you want them to.

Mirrored Body Language

They say one of the sincerest forms of flattery is mimicry, and this remains true when it comes to body language. If someone is mirroring your body language, this indicates they are engaged with you and are interested in the experience you are sharing. It also indicates that they feel secure, trusting, and comfortable with you, which are all excellent qualities for a person to experience during sales.

When your client does this, it means they are feeling engaged with everything you are saying, and they are excited to learn more. You can feel confident that a person will purchase through you if you see they are mirroring your body language. You can also encourage a person to mirror your body language by mirroring theirs, as this gets their subconscious mind focused and can bring them into that active state of engagement.

When you do this, you show your client that you are like them. In their subconscious mind, they realize you are not scary or unsuspecting but that you are similar to them and, therefore, safe and predictable. This means their skepticism and fear-barriers will be broken as they learn to trust you and accept what you are sharing with them.

To mirror someone properly, you do not want to do exactly what they are doing. Instead, you want to copy *some* of their moves. When they cross their legs, for example, you might cross yours within 30 seconds after that. Or, if they move their hand in a certain way, you might complete a similar movement a few seconds later. Only do this a few times, not consistently; otherwise, you will look odd. If you do it sparingly, but in a way that is recognizable by their subconscious mind, you will get that client on the same page as you and will have a much higher success rate when it comes to closing deals.

Consistent Eye Contact

Eye contact is a wonderful indicator of how things are going, especially in sales. Through eye contact, you gain the ability to "see" into what someone thinks and how they feel. Adequate eye contact will affect you and your prospect, so it is important to be aware of how to read this type of body language and how to use it to your advantage.

When your client does this, consistent eye contact means they are interested and actively processing what you have to say. While people will often gaze off in the distance from time to time to process the information you have shared, consistent eye contact at various points throughout the conversation is important. The more a person makes eye contact with you, the more confident and connected they are feeling, and the more likely they are to stay engaged with you throughout the sale.

When you do this, it shows your client that you are engaged and that you care. People that fail to make consistent eye contact, or that actively avoid it are often seen as having something to hide, which causes others to become untrusting and skeptical. Regularly look at your client, but avoid staring. Instead, look intently, but look away every so often to break the gaze and create balance overall.

An excellent way to make eye contact is to do it whenever you or your client is talking, but look away when they gesture to something or begin making hand gestures. Look at their physical movements, as well as the product or service you are selling, and then look back to them. Keeping your eyes moving, but focused on them and the contents of the sales experience is an excellent way to provide generous eye contact without seeming as though you are staring.

Intentional Facial Expressions

Facial expressions are an important part of body language. They say a lot about what someone thinks or feels. In every conversation you have, you use your face to communicate with other people, and they use theirs to communicate with you. Being intentional about reading facial expressions is a great opportunity to be aware of what someone else is saying to you and you to them, so you can say all the right things to land a sale.

When your client does this, be aware of what specific facial expressions they are using. Their eyes, the movement of their mouth, their cheeks, nose, forehead, and even neck all provide insight as to what they are thinking and feeling. Generally speaking, a face that is light and rested indicates someone is relaxed and feeling casual. A face that is scrunched forward indicates anger or disgust, and a face that is stretched outward with raised eyebrows and a dropped jaw indicates surprise or shock.

When you do this, your facial expressions should be used as a way to communicate authority and friendliness. You want to smile, keep soft eyes, and maintain a resting face, but keep a look of confidence to yourself. The easiest way to practice the look of confidence is to go to your bathroom mirror, get in a confident mood, and look at yourself. Then, practice making that face on a regular basis. Using this face, alongside a genuine smile and a welcoming look, is an excellent way to create a comfortable environment for your client.

Arms and Torso

Your upper body communicates more than you likely think it does. Being aware of what your upper body is saying is a great way to communicate intentionally, rather than unintentionally. Because your upper body accounts for so much of your overall being, and it is often elaborate in gestures, it is an important part of communication. Be aware of what your arms and torso are saying, and look at your client to see what theirs are saying, too.

When your client does this, pay attention to where their arms are and what direction their torso is facing. If their arms are to the side or actively engaged, and their torso is facing you, this indicates they are with you. Their facial expressions and words can help you determine if they are with you in a positive way or a negative way. Naturally, you want them to be with you in a positive way. If your client's arms are crossed, are hanging limp down by their sides, or are behind their back as they clasp their hands behind them, this indicates they are disinterested or not with you. For their torso, if they are leaning toward you, this is a good sign that they are focused and interested in what you have to say. If they are learning away, they are skeptical, disinterested, or getting ready to end the conversation.

When you do this, you want to keep active gestures that are not excessive or overwhelming. Use your hands to communicate or keep them calmly rested in your lap, on your desk, or somewhere else casual. Lean in slightly, and keep your torso pointed toward the person you are talking to, as this creates a sense of interest and connection. When a person feels as though you are addressing them personally, they are far more likely to listen and care about what you have to say.

Legs and Feet

Lastly, you need to pay attention to the legs and feet. Our legs and feet do communicate a lot, though they are not looked at as often as our upper bodies since they are lower and are generally beyond the field of view when we are in active conversation. Because your legs are less noticeable, you do not have to be quite so focused on them; however, it does help to pay attention so you can add to the overall communication.

When your client does this, the best thing you can do is to pay attention to their feet. Their feet will give you the best information instantly, and without you needing to look down for terribly long. All you need to do is focus on where their feet are pointing, as this tells you what they are most interested in. If their feet are pointed toward you or the product you are selling them, this is a sign that they are engaged with you and are interested in what you have to say. If they are pointed away, especially toward the exit, this means they are looking for a way to end the conversation so they can leave.

When you do this, you should also only worry about keeping your legs neat and your feet pointed in the direction of your interest. In this case, you want to keep at least one foot pointed toward your client, which indicates you are engaged with them. While your client is highly unlikely to consciously recognize this, their subconscious brain will become aware and will use this as a positive cue to indicate a greater sense of security, trust, and connection.

CHAPTER 14
Use Redirections As Often As Needed

Redirections are a tactic that allows you to take the present situation and redirect it toward where you want it to go. This is an excellent course-correction tool that helps you keep things on track without coming across as sleazy, pushy, or like your only focus is on making the sale. Of course, your number one focus is on closing the deal, but if you are doing it right, you are also invested in creating an excellent experience and honoring your client in the process. Effective redirection strategies allow you to guide your client toward the original topic so you can keep your client on the same page as you and reach your objective in the most direct way possible.

Avoid Becoming Confrontational

The most important thing to be aware of when it comes to redirections is the possibility for them to become confrontational. Redirecting your client back to the primary topic can seem confrontational if you are continually pressuring them back to the original topic and not giving the conversation room to flow freely. You need to be willing to communicate about what you want and what your client wants; otherwise, they feel as though you have only confronted them to demand they give you your way. This is not a good situation to be in, and can often lead to angry clients that never close a sale with you because they feel as though they have not been respected throughout the process.

Another form of confrontation to be aware of in redirections is the way you come across during objection redirections. If someone tells you they cannot afford what you have, and you say, "I'm sure you can," you are confrontational. You have to redirect in a way that is compassionate, shows consideration for the person's objection, and provides them an alternative that allows them to honor that objection while also doing what you want them to do.

Redirect to Get Back on Topic

As you go through a sales conversation, it can be easy for things to get off-topic. Particularly during the warm-up phase, when you are getting to know your client, it can be easy to fixate on the details of who they are and lose sight of the real reason you are there. At least, for them, it is. For you, you may be sitting there wondering when the best opportunity is to get them focused on the sale and considering when they will make the purchase from you.

Redirecting a conversation to get it back on the topic should be done in a casual way, and after you have given the other person a few minutes to talk about themselves and their own experiences. When people talk about themselves, they feel good, so you want to encourage this. To effectively redirect these conversations, you can use a point they made and direct it toward the sale you are making, which naturally redirects the conversation to the sale while making it seem like you are still talking about the client.

For example:
- "No way, you have a six-year-old? My six year old loves this product, I'll bet yours will, too!"
- "That sounds like hard work to do, and it would definitely be easier if you had these new boots."
- "That sounds like a beautiful trip; I can see why you would like a larger vehicle for the next one! Have you seen the cargo space in our minivans?"
- "Wow, what an inspiring story. I understand why you want to treat yourself! This is the perfect product for that."

Getting conversations back on topic this way is seamless, easy, and will support you with creating the opportunity to get back to your pitch. This way, your sale does not drag on or end up with you and your client becoming so distracted that you never get to finalize the sale.

Redirect Your Client Through Objections

Your client is inevitably going to have objections. You will likely see statistics such as 9 out of 10 people have objections, and you have to work through those objections to help them make the purchase. The easiest way through objections is with the use of redirections. The four most common objections are a lack of interest, contentment, budget, and time. If your client says, "I'm not interested," you might ask, "What are you currently using?" This way, you get insight into what they are using and can make comparisons or educate them on why your product or service is better than what they already have. As such, you end up closing far more sales.

If your client says, "I'm happy with my current system," you might say, "How long have you been using your current system?" This allows you to gain more information from your client, such as how the system has helped them and if there are any weaknesses, which gives you the opportunity to pitch your product as the solution.

If your client says, "I don't have the budget," you might say I completely understand. I'm not seeking to sell or suggest any changes today. My goal is just to open a conversation to learn more and share information." This way, you make it clear that you are asking for a bit of their time to understand what they are already using, and to let them know another solution is available. Then, when the finances become available, they are far more likely to reach out and take you up on your offer.

If your client says, "I don't have the time," you might say, "I completely understand. When would be the most convenient time for me to reach out to you?" Which gives you the opportunity to make a clearly defined follow-up opportunity, where you can then follow up and hopefully make a sale!

Working through objections with redirections gives you the opportunity to keep the conversation going, which means you can keep the sale potential open. If you let the conversation end after one objective, you will lose out on many sales because you have let them slide too easy. You must be willing to work with clients through their objectives to show them the possibilities; otherwise, you are cutting yourself short.

Redirect Yourself to Your Confidence

Experiencing temporary blows to your confidence is common, but when it happens during a sale, it can cause you to bomb. Naturally, you do not want to blow a sale, so you need to figure out how to redirect yourself so you can get back to your element of confidence. A quick, effortless way to redirect yourself to confidence is to have a mantra you repeat in your mind that reminds you why you are here, why you are doing this, and why you chose to be confident and shameless in the first place.

Before you get into sales, repeat this mantra to yourself and give yourself a few minutes to think about all the things it means to you. Then, during an active sale, repeat it as often as needed to keep your head in the game and your focus on the outcome.

Some great mantras you might use include:
- "I'm doing this for _____."
- "Be interested to be interesting."
- "24 Hours to Celebrate or Wallow in Misery."
- "Make it happen."
- "I choose YES."

These mantras can quickly be repeated to yourself in your mind, and can drive you to maintain your confidence as long as it is needed. If you need to, pause to have a drink of water and repeat your mantra in your mind as you go through the sale. You will be far more successful if you redirect yourself to confidence than you will be if you let yourself stumble and stay down. If you become efficient with this, your clients will never even notice your stumble.

CHAPTER 15
Research People And Get To Know Them

The best way to get what you want from someone is to be informed about what they want to get from you. As you know, sales are best made when you are selling someone something they want or need, in a way they want it. The sale is as much about your client as it is about you, which is why you need to remain focused on them as much as possible.

An excellent way to reach your client and make the largest impact on them is to research people and get to know who they are on a deeper level. If you are new to sales, this process may seem strange or unusual, but it is actually one of the most natural things you can do. In fact, you already do it in your regular, everyday life. Learning to do it for sales only requires a slight shift and the addition of one extra step, which will make your research process far easier.

The extra step is basic: you research your lead demographic, not just the individual person you are selling to. Most of the people in your target audience will be of the same one to three demographics. Researching these demographics and their needs and preferences relating to what you have for sale, and otherwise, is an excellent way to understand your client in a deeper way. This way, you can use this understanding to recognize the needs of your clients, generate value around your offer, and make the connection regarding how your offer fulfills their needs.

Aside from this extra step, the rest of your research process is basic. This is the same process you use in your everyday life when you are getting to know new friends. Your research consists of asking questions, getting to know the individual, and coming to understand their unique take on the problem they are having. This way, when you pitch the solution, you pitch it in a way that meets their unique needs.

The biggest mind manipulation hack here is that when a person feels like you truly know and understand them, they are far more likely to trust you and the guidance you offer. As they face this problem, they look to you to be an authoritative figure with the solution, and they will happily follow your guidance *if* they believe you are the right authority for them. This is an effortless perspective to create when you have an existing basic understanding of who they are, plus the added time spent getting to know them and their needs.

Researching Your Lead Demographic

During the selling process, you have a finite amount of time to get to know someone. Unlike with new friendships, you do not generally have hours upon hours to listen to what someone has to say; instead, you have an hour or less to get to know that person enough to be able to confidently sell them a solution to their troubles. The easiest way to get to know someone quickly, and establish rapport by expressing a sense of all-knowing compassion for their troubles, is to have a basic understanding of your lead demographic. In some cases, you might have as many as three lead demographics or groups of people that are most likely to purchase through you. Researching each of your three leading demographics ensures you have a clear understanding of these three archetypes, which you can then use to lay the foundation on the research process with each new client.

Before you begin researching your demographic, you have to know who they are. If you are working privately, pay close attention to who is responding most to your content to the point of purchasing through you. If you work with a company, pay attention to their online presence to get a better idea of who is interacting most with their company and purchasing through them. It can also be helpful to look at your direct competition to see who their demographic is, as you will have similar demographics. Focus not only on likes and comments but on reviews which indicate that someone has actually purchased through the company at some point. This is important, as many demographics will show interest in your company, but only specific ones will actually purchase. In business, you care more about your purchasing demographic than anyone else.

Once you know who your demographic is, you need to get to know the basics about who these individuals are. Start by answering simple identifying questions like:
- Who are they?
- Where do they live?
- How old are they?
- What is their income level?
- Are they married?
- Do they drive?

These questions give you a general idea of the client avatar you are focused on selling to. However, you should not stop there. You should also look deeper into researching aspects of that person that is related to you and your product or service.
- What are their pain points?
- What are their primary struggles?
- What do they need more of?
- What do they need less of?
- What issues do they have that seem irrelevant to your offer, but that have a surprising or unexpected link to your solution?
- What drives them to purchase something?
- What do they need from you?
- What type of sales experience do they enjoy?
- What do they absolutely not enjoy?

- What will make them take out their wallet and purchase from you?

Obviously, the exact answers to these questions will vary from person to person, but the general answers will remain the same throughout your demographic. For this reason, you want to answer these initial questions accurately, but not overly descriptively. Leave room for you to remain curious so you can research how each individual client matches that description and build from there.

Warming Up Clients With Personal Research

During the sales process, there is a warming up phase where you get to know your client, and they get to know you. This is where you ask questions, seek to understand what needs they have, and start recognizing ways that your offer can fulfill their needs. It is important that you do your research thoroughly at this point, as effective research here will ensure that you are able to later ask for the sale in a way that will almost guarantee you a positive result. If you do not do due diligence here, you may walk into the ask completely blind to what is needed, and therefore struggling to make it happen. The number of rejections you get will be unreasonably high because you did not take the time to truly understand the need of your client and meet that need for them.

Doing personal research on your clients means you need to be asking questions like:
- "Can I ask you some questions about your _____?"
- "Tell me more about your experience with _____?"
- "You specialize in _____. Why did you choose that niche?"
- "What are your goals for the next ___ months?"
- "Why is this a priority for you right now?"
- "What are your priorities right now?"
- "Are you using anything like this already?"
- "Can you give me some background information about your experience with _____?"
- "What do you do?"
- "What projects are you currently working on?"
- "Do you have a budget in mind?"
- "What is your buying criteria for this?"
- "Are there other people involved in your purchasing process?"

These types of questions help you learn more about your individual prospect, which gives you more significant insight into their wants and needs. You can layer this over your existing understanding of their demographic and use it all to your advantage when it comes to pitching your offer in a way that sounds like what they truly desire.

It is worth noting that what you learn about a prospect from their own words always trumps what you learn about them through their demographic. While you can use demographic-oriented knowledge to create a more dynamic understanding of who they are, you should always believe what they say about themselves to be true. This way, you pitch to the individual and not your demographic as a whole. General demographics only matter in marketing, individual demographic matters in sales.

Using Your Research to Define Your Sales Objectives

Your research provides you with everything you need to define your sales objectives, so long as you have been thorough. By the end of your warm-up, you should know what your client needs, why, and how they are going to get it. You should also be aware of what you need to do in order to meet their needs, and how you can adjust your approach to create a positive experience for them. If you know everything you need to know to pitch your offer and receive a yes, then you have done thorough research.

The last step is to define how you will connect your client to the offer, so they are most likely to say yes. To do this, you need to recall their need, identify no more than three to five ways your offer helps them meet this need, and discover how you can outline these values so that your client sees the value in your offer, too. It is important that you never offer more than five reasons, and that these reasons are individualized to that person because doing so can overwhelm your client. Realistically, three value-packed reasons are plenty to encourage your client to see the value, and the two additional reasons can be reserved for clients that need a little extra encouragement.

Once you can clearly see the connection between the offer and the client's needs, all you have to do is wait for the right moment to make your pitch. Usually, the right moment follows you, discovering all of this information, which makes tracking it and taking advantage of it extremely simple!

CHAPTER 16
Right Timing, Right Opportunity

Aligning your offer with the right timing and right opportunity is imperative if you want to be successful in sales. To take this a step further and really tap into the values of mind manipulation, focus on having the right timing and right opportunity for your follow up, too. Every client has a sweet spot for when they say yes, and some may fall after your initial contact, which is why follow-ups are so important. Learning to master the timing is the best way to make sure you get your yes.

Timing the follow up is especially important because you want to come back while a person still has you, and your offer, in mind. You also want to come back at a point where they are more likely to say yes, which is usually within a few days, or maybe a couple of weeks at most. Avoid letting follow-ups sit too long, as doing so can cost you sales. Your timing should come across as helpful with a friendly reminder, rather than pushy or so late that you have to re-pitch the entire offer because your client has already forgotten about the thrill of the idea.

Understand the Problem First

Perhaps the most important timing concern is regarding your level of compassionate understanding of your client's needs. If you do not yet understand their problem, you do not have enough information to sell them anything. Give yourself time to ask probing questions that allow you to deepen your understanding, and your client time to answer these questions thoroughly. From your questions and their answers, you should have a clear understanding of their objectives and what problems are preventing them from reasonably achieving those objectives.

It is essential that you avoid showing up and giving too much information at once, as this overwhelms people and prevents them from purchasing. Further, it leads to you emphasizing points that may be entirely irrelevant to your client, while ignoring ones that may be essential to their decision. Rather than pulling a "show up and throw up," focus on showing up and listening. This way, you have a greater opportunity to listen to their needs and thoroughly understand why your offer can help them fulfill those needs.

Understand the Value of the Problem

It is not enough to merely understand what the problem is; you must also understand how significantly the problem is impacting your client. Fully grasping the scale to which this problem is affecting your client allows you to emphasize the most valuable features, while also really selling that these are the features they need to resolve their problems. Learning about the extent of their problems makes it sound like you are genuinely compassionate toward your client and what they are struggling with, which you should be. However, it also helps you thoroughly understand the value of your offer and how your offer can benefit your client.

As a salesperson, you know your offer is valuable and that everyone wants or needs it in one way or another. However, you must understand *why* each person wants or needs it if you will become successful in selling it. For example, let's say you are selling a loaf of bread. If you were selling that loaf of bread to someone that is exceptionally hungry, the selling point might be that it is good quality food for cheap. Alternatively, if you were selling that bread to someone that likes luxurious things, your selling point may be that it is made with high-quality, organic ingredients and offers a delicious culinary experience.

You must understand the value your client needs, and how your solution fulfills that value, if you will successfully sell your products to others. Never make your pitch before you can respect the extent to which your client's problems are troubling them, so you know the value of your offer and what it will truly provide your client with.

Slow Down Your Sales Process

If you rush to the finish line, your sales process will suck, and your results will be exceptionally poor. People do not want to be rushed, especially when it comes to deciding how they should spend their hard-earned money. If you want to speed up your sales, you must start by slowing your sales down as much as possible. Be generous with your time as you get to know a new prospect, be open to discussion, and be persistent with your approach. The more time you take with someone, the more you get to understand them and make a sales approach that suits their purchasing style, which means they will have a thoroughly enjoyable experience working with you. When you treat a person like you have all day, it rarely takes them more than a few minutes to make a decision to purchase with you. However, if you treat someone like they only have five minutes, they will be unlikely to purchase through you at all.

An excellent way to make sure you are giving the sales process enough time is to consider the amount of knowledge you have about your client. You should have a concrete idea of how they make their decisions, what their time frame looks like, and if they have already budgeted to make said purchase with you. If you do not know the answer to these three questions, you are likely rushing through the sales process. You should feel excited about the solution and absolutely confident in how the solution will serve this individual; otherwise, you may be rushing the sale.

Remain in Control With Timing

This is where the mind manipulation tactics related to timing come into significant effect. Even though you are honoring the timelines of your client and looking to make them feel in control, you want to be the one that is genuinely in control over the timing. You can remain in control of timing by actively recognizing where your client is in their purchasing process, and by staying one step ahead of them so you can direct them through the experience. Remember, even if you establish strong rapport, you are still a stranger to your client, so you must value them and their right to choose, and take their time, if they will trust you and purchase with you. The same goes for asking anything of anyone, whether it is sales-related or not.

If you are selling products or services that are under about one hundred dollars, the timing of the sale can usually be brought to completion within the day. Once you see the right emotional response, which is excitement and need, cross your clients' face, you know you are ready to pitch the sale. If you are selling a product or service that is worth significantly more than about a hundred dollars, it is important to recognize that very few people will be ready to spend that type of money right away. Chances are, they will want to come back one to two more times to discuss the purchase before following through, as they want to think about it, budget for it, and ensure that they purchase it when the time is right for them. If you honor this, you remain in control.

As you look across your product suite, get to know which products and services are most likely to sell without much thought, which will require more thought, and which will require the most. Then, anticipate spending more time on those that will require the most thought, since these are ones that people need time to process before purchasing. If you allot enough time for each sale process, you won't rush the experience, and you'll be able to ask for the sale when the timing is perfect for the client.

If your client does need more than a few minutes to make their purchase, make sure you acknowledge that and tell them how to spend their time. For example, if you know someone will generally need to look at an expensive television twice before purchasing it, on average, following your first point of contact you should tell your client when to come back to look at it again. Telling them when to come back, or encouraging them to bring back the other person related to their purchasing decisions, means they now have the desire in their mind to follow through. As long as you say so casually, and after establishing positive rapport, people will always appreciate being told what to do.

You might say something like:

- "I'll be back on Friday, so why don't you take some time to think it over and crunch some numbers, then come back, and we can discuss it then?"
- "If your (wife/husband/partner/roommate/etc.) is available Sunday, why not come back then so we can all discuss it and see if it is the right fit?"
- "We have a sale starting Tuesday. Why not take some time to think it over, then come back and see if you can get it at a better deal?"

These are all excellent ways to casually suggest someone take your desired action, without making it seem as though you are bossing them around. Remember, if you come in and tell a complete stranger what they ought to be doing, you are the one with the real problem, not them. Even if they tell you what their problems are, you still need to remain focused on guiding but not forcing, because your clients need the freedom to make their own choices as they see fit.

Time It for the Client, Not Yourself

When you do reach the point where you are ready to ask for the sale, you must be confident that you have timed it for the clients' level of readiness, and not your level of need. Asking a client to make a purchase because you think they are ready is an excellent way to ask too soon. Asking when they are ready is the perfect way to ask at the time when you are most likely to hear "yes."

If you are walking away from your first meeting with a client, book your second meeting now. Do not wait, and do not accept a commitment to call you to book a meeting. Book a meeting now and invite them to reschedule if they need to, which ensures that the meeting is in the books and ready to go. Inviting your client to book a meeting means they can tell you when they would be ready to discuss this topic again, which is excellent for their purchasing objectives. This way, you know you are not rushing it or waiting too long; you are doing everything on your clients' terms. When it comes time to make the sale, be as thorough and generous as you have been the entire time, and you will be far more likely to achieve phenomenal results.

CHAPTER 17
Expand Your Mind Power

Fixating on how you can progress in sales without ever focusing on your personal development is like fixating on how you can become more fit without ever physically engaging in exercise. You cannot expand your sales knowledge and success without expanding the overall power of your mind, which is your most valuable asset. You must discover how you can activate the fullest potential of your mind so you can rely on it to help you approach new clients, get to know them, pitch them, and close the sale. Because you will come across so many types of people and so many objectives, the more you can rely on your mind, the stronger your results will be.

Another value of being able to rely on your mind power is that adequate control over your mind means you do not have to worry about your own experiences holding you back. For example, if you have a bad day, experience a rejection, or bomb a meeting with someone important, excellent mind power means that you can continue into your next sale without holding that negative experience up as your own personal obstacle. Rather than letting it define you or affect your next experience, you set it aside and focus completely on engaging with your new client and moving into your new order of business. Later, you can reflect on those experiences and look for a growth opportunity, but in the meantime, you can stay in control and focus on your next objective.

Invoke the Power of Meditation and Visualization

Meditation and visualization are top tools that virtually every successful person uses to one degree or another. Some set aside time to meditate and visualize daily, while others only do it as needed, such as before important events or meetings. Using the power of meditation and visualization to your advantage means you can regulate yourself and your stress, develop focus and expand your self-control.

Studies have shown that those who meditate daily build their emotional resistance, gain greater control over their emotions, and increase their self-awareness and awareness overall. Some of the most successful people meditate at the start of their day and immediately before important events to ensure that they are grounded, in control, and in their element so they can succeed at anything they engage in.

As you meditate, resolve to keep your focus on your breath. Thoughts will come and go, emotions may surface, and you might find yourself feeling fidgety or like you need to physically get up and move around, but this is where your moment of power comes in. If you can continually redirect your focus to your breath and breathe through all of these thoughts, feelings, and distracting urges, your self-control will rapidly develop. It is this self-control that will aid you in relying on yourself and creating your desired results in sales, and any other form of mind manipulation you may engage in.

Visualization is equally as powerful, giving your brain the illusion that you have already completed something even if you haven't. For example, if you visualize that you enter a sales call and succeed, your brain will believe this has already happened. The more you visualize it, the more confidence you will feel, and the easier it will be for you to step into sales calls with that same level of confidence and focus. Research has shown that visualizing for just 10 minutes a day can completely transform your brain and provide you with the mental strength to make the results you desire.

As you visualize, focus on bringing as many elements into your visualization as possible. Do not just visualize what you want, bring as many senses into the experience as possible, provide context, and behave as though you are recalling a memory, even if it is a memory of the future. Visualize the taste, smell, feel, sight, and sound of success, and yourself engaging with these senses, too. What will be said to you, and what will you say back? What perfume or cologne will you be wearing, or what other smells might be associated with the experience? What will you see? What will they see? Are there any physical sensations you can become aware of? What feelings are you experiencing emotionally? Provide context for the visualization, and everything happening in it. Why is it happening? What does it represent? How did you get there? The more detailed you are, the more powerful your visualizations will be, and the more success you will generate.

Play Puzzle Games That Are Problem-Oriented

Mind manipulation relies heavily on your ability to solve problems. You need to solve the problems of others so you can coerce them to solve your problem, too. In sales, for example, you need to solve their problem with your product so they can solve your problem by making a purchase. Because you gave them a solution to their troubles, they gave you a sale so you would get closer to your objective. Of course, they don't see it that way, but that is how it works.

Playing puzzle games that are problem-oriented is a great way to expand your mind power around problem-solving. The more efficient you are with solving problems, the faster you will be able to solve another person's problem and discover how you can present the solution in an enticing manner. These games will also help you work through objectives and move your client toward desiring what you have to offer, which makes sales far easier for you.

Beyond increasing your problem-solving abilities, puzzles help you expand your concentration, increase your attention to detail, improve your memory, and become more productive. These are all excellent traits to have in sales, as they allow you to focus on your clients' needs, identify the exact value you can offer them, and recall why that value is so important to them when it is time to pitch.

Take Care of Your Physical Wellness

Caring for your physical wellness actually carries a three-fold benefit when it comes to sales. Firstly, it expands your mind power by offering your brain the care it requires to function at its fullest capacity. Second, it enables you to feel good about yourself, and when you feel good, you show up differently. Third, caring for your physical wellness makes you look better overall, which means people will be more inspired by you and more likely to listen to you and trust you. After all, a person that looks like they take good care of themselves is far more attractive and convincing than a person that looks sleep-deprived, starved, and in need of a good stretch.

To take proper care of your body, focus on your physical, mental, and emotional health. Physically, eat right, move your body, mind your hygiene, and get adequate rest. Mentally, engage in frequent stress-relieving activities, read, do puzzles, and challenge your mind on a regular basis. Emotionally, release your emotions as needed, talk to people, hire a therapist, and do what you need to in order to work through your feelings. The more balanced you can keep yourself in every way possible, the more you will be able to rely on yourself, and the more stable you will come across in sales meetings.

Expand Your Emotional Intelligence

Emotional intelligence is an essential element of mind power, and sales. When you have excellent emotional intelligence, your self-awareness improves your own emotional management, as well as your ability to manage others emotionally. Being able to do both will not only increase your fulfillment from life, but also support you with navigating the many trials and tribulations of sales conversations.

You can expand your emotional intelligence, or EQ, by meditating, asserting yourself, reflecting on your emotions, discovering how to maintain an optimistic attitude, and motivating yourself to stay in control of yourself. There are several excellent books written about emotional intelligence which can support you with increasing your skill in this particular area of your life.

In sales, emotional intelligence is especially important as it affects how you carry yourself and the level of control you have over the sale. When you have excellent self-awareness, you can prevent your own emotions from becoming a hindrance to your sales process. Rather than letting fear, concern, or worry drive your motives, you can keep yourself focused on creating a positive, fulfilling experience for all involved. You can also prevent yourself from carrying stress from other parts of your day into the sales call, all of which can damage your performance. Since emotional intelligence also includes your ability to manage other people's emotions, this means you also gain the ability to guide your client's emotions in a positive direction, so they are receptive during your sales pitch.

Invest in the Other Seven Areas of Your Life

Stress serves as a significant hindrance to people's success. If you are stressed, you will not be performing at your peak function. You must learn how to manage your stress by discovering how you can invest in and nurture the other seven areas of your life, beyond work. According to the wheel of life, aside from work, you also have the following categories in your life: wealth, health, relationships, romance, relationship to self, hobbies, and faith. If you invest abundantly into making all areas of your life more enjoyable, you not only experience a well-rounded life, but you also find it easier to show up to different areas of your life. Due to your abundant feelings of fulfillment, you do not have worries or feelings of inadequacy or lack of plaguing you from other areas of your life. Deep-seated joy and contentment are far more attractive and magnetizing than being someone that is only partially fulfilled.

This means that, if you want to abundantly invest in your success with mind manipulation and sales, you also need to abundantly invest in things that fulfill you elsewhere in life. Spend time with loved ones, invest in your marriage or love life, learn to love yourself, manage your finances, take care of your health, invest in activities you genuinely enjoy, and develop your faith in whatever you might believe in, religious or otherwise. The more you invest in these areas of your life, the more well-rounded your life will be and the better you will be at everything you do.

CHAPTER 18
Always Have A Positive Desire

One of the surest ways to hold yourself back or stumble upon your success is to fear that you are doing something to harm another individual. If you, in any way, believe that through your mind manipulation strategies you are harming another person, you will hold yourself back through a natural inhibition that prevents you from hurting others'. We all have this inhibition to varying degrees, and it stunts us from ever doing something that could hurt another human. At the end of the day, we all want to see everyone win.

Though we have already discussed the importance of perspective to creating a positive experience, I want to dig deeper into this so you genuinely feel positive about your mind manipulation strategies. First and foremost, remember that your desire is not to force someone into doing something they don't want; rather, you want to encourage them to see the value in something they do want or need. When you can clearly see how your product, service, or offer would benefit another person, your entire focus, then, is on showing them how they can see it the same way. This way, they gain access to the benefits you are providing them with, and you both win.

Look to Inform, Not Sell

An excellent way to rapidly shift your perspective to one that values a positive experience for all is to focus on informing, not selling. If you get into a conversation with the intention of selling, you will likely feel as though you have to do whatever it takes to force that person to buy from you. This is where you find yourself feeling as though you are doing something hurtful to that person, and where your tactics must be inhibited to prevent you from following through with a harmful process. Rather than fixating on making a sale, focus on informing the other person. This way, rather than trying to sell something to them, you are simply informing them of an opportunity that is available that can help them experience greater success in any given area of their lives. The benefit of this focus is that you are genuinely focused on helping them from start to finish. You are not there attempting to coerce them into a sale by being helpful with the intention of using that to snag results. Instead, you are there to offer help and allow them to decide whether the amount to which you helped is worth their investment or not. This way, the entire decision is out of your hands and into theirs, so you have no need to carry any level of guilt or concern around the way you showed up to that sales conversation.

The benefit of showing up only to help and inform is that you never create the feeling of being "sold to." People generally do not enjoy this feeling because they worry they will buy into a gimmick or something that will not genuinely help them. Rather than making them feel sold to, you want to make everyone you help feel served. Let them worry about the sale, and you will almost always earn a positive response.

Genuinely Avoid Ill-Fit Individuals

If you are selling to everyone, then you are selling nothing. With marketing in particular, it is well-known that if you try to sell to everyone, you will overwhelm your marketing strategy and fail to get to anyone. Instead, you need to be highly specific about who you are talking to and focus on only talking to that individual. This is why businesses are always niching down and focusing on their core demographic, because this way they are speaking directly to a specific individual, and they are creating results because of it. Sure, people from other demographics may discover their product and purchase it, and eventually, they will expand out to different demographics, but they gain their results because they know their demographic so well. The same can be said for sales.

When you know exactly who you are talking to, you feel confident that you are only ever talking to the right people. This way, you are not wasting anyone's time or trying to encourage an ill-fit person to purchase your products. Instead, you are focused exclusively on selling products that are needed by a certain type of person, to that person.

If you come across someone that seems ill-fit and they want to discuss the sale, follow their guidance. You should never tell someone not to buy something; this should merely guide you away from intentionally targeting the wrong people. Should someone come to you interested in learning about what you have to offer, assume they are a good fit and focus on informing them, just as you would with any other client. This way, if they do decide they are a good fit, they can go ahead and purchase your product. If they don't, they may know someone that better fits your target demographic, and they can recommend that individual to you so you earn another sale. Never make assumptions about people, or what they want or need. Trust the process.

It's Your Duty to Make the Offer

If you are worried about how someone will receive your offer, consider this: is it really your job to make the decision for them? No. Your job as a sales person, whether you are selling a product, service, or selling your vision to someone so you can achieve your dreams, is to present the opportunity. It is the other person's job to decide whether they want to take it or not. If you make the assumption for them, you are essentially deciding on their behalf and robbing them of the opportunity to say yes and receive the valuable offer you had for them.

Think about it this way, if you were a waitress, would you skip giving a menu to a paying customer and instead bring them what you assumed they wanted, regardless of whether you assumed right or not? No. This would be heinous, as you would likely assume wrong, and the other person would be tremendously frustrated that you never gave them the opportunity in the first place. The same goes for sales. Your job is not to make a decision for someone; it is to let them know that there is a decision to be made in the first place, and to inform them of the varying reasons as to why making that decision would be a good idea.

When it comes to selling, we automatically think people will not want to hear from us or receive our offers because we are afraid they might say no. We don't want to take up space, waste people's time, or make them feel disrespected by us, so instead we assume they don't want to hear from us altogether. This is rarely the case. People are always open to hearing what you have to say, as long as you say it at the right time and with the right intention. Ensure that you approach someone during a respectable time, and come back at a time they agree to if they need, and make the offer from a genuine place of service. Through this, you are focused on giving them the opportunity, rather than making the decision for them one way or another. This is far more positive in nature than assuming, and likely assuming wrong in the process.

Be Honest and Explain Your Process

An excellent way to feel good about sales and to keep a positive desire in mind is to be transparent with everyone you share with. Be honest about what you know and don't know, and about what your objectives are. If you are asked questions about anything relating to what you are doing, be honest in your answer. Honesty is a wonderful way to build rapport, increase trust, and encourage people to feel good about doing business with you, while increasing your good feelings, too.

It can also be helpful to explain your process, which allows people to anticipate what you are sharing with them. Let people know that you will first seek to understand how you can help them; then you will let them know of ways that you can help them. Then, if they desire, they can choose to receive that help or not. This is an excellent time to emphasize your focus on being helpful and offering support, rather than your focus on making a sale. Let them know that your number one objective is to assist them in having a positive experience in a specific area of their life, and invite them to the experience with you.

You must understand that the days of having pushy salespeople that sell through confusion and mysticism are over. You are not trying to hide any details, bury the lead, or keep the truth away from someone. It is fine to say that your desire is to make a sale, but more than that, your desire is to see if you can help them enjoy a better quality of life. The more honest you are, the more people will trust you and the better the sales process will feel, as you are being genuine and with integrity.

CONCLUSION

Congratulations on completing *Mind Manipulation for Beginners!* This book was written to assist you with understanding mind manipulation, and discovering how you can effectively manipulate anyone to do what you want them to do. While we focused on sales and business, mind manipulation can be used to sell anything to anyone. If you want to encourage your friends to eat at your favorite restaurant, your parents to make a specific dinner for the holidays, or your spouse to take a certain business trip with you, these are excellent techniques to use. There are countless ways that you can sell your offers to people, all of which can improve the quality of your life. The more you learn to sell using these tactics, the better your results will be.

I hope that, after reading this, you discover that mind manipulation is not nearly as challenging as you may have once thought, and it can be done in an entirely ethical manner. Your objective should never be to get what you desire at all costs; rather, to align yourself with people that will get you where you want to go. By releasing your attachment on who, and instead focusing on how, you make room for the right people to show up so you can meet your objectives. You also do this in a way that feels positive for everyone involved.

After you read this book, I encourage you to start using these tactics in your real, everyday life. It may be useful to start in low-pressure environments, such as encouraging your partner to take you out for coffee on a certain day, or your friends to do what you want to do next weekend, rather than what they want to do. However, there is no reason to hold yourself back and jump into a low-pressure environment if you don't want to. If you thrive by jumping off the deep end and learning through hands-on experience, go straight to using these strategies in your future sales calls. Watch how significantly your results change when you work with peoples' minds to manipulate your desired results and how positive everyone feels in the end. Not only will you get your way, but people will be happy to oblige you, too.

Remember, there is no reason why you should not desire what you do. Your wants and needs are appropriate, and you deserve to ask to have them fulfilled. If you desire to make a sale, then make it. The worst that will happen is someone genuinely says no, and then you move on to another person. Be consistent, develop your confidence, and acknowledge your deservingness to fulfill your needs. Every single one of us has them, and every one of us deserves to do what we need to in order to meet them. With sales, you need to make sales to make money, and you need that money to take care of your family or support your dreams. There is absolutely nothing wrong with that.

The more you expand your emotional intelligence, and your mind power overall, the easier it will be to develop your confidence and purpose behind your approach. This way, you are manipulating from a solid foundation, which will lead to greater results. Rooting yourself deeply in confidence, purpose, and a strong desire to serve everyone's best interest will always work to your benefit. Motivate yourself to be the best in all areas of your life, and you will inevitably become the best in the areas you care about most.

Before you go, I wanted to ask one favor. If you could please go to Amazon and review *Mind Manipulation for Beginners,* I would appreciate it. Your honest review will help others just like you discover how they can improve their mind manipulation skills and become excellent sales people, too. Through this, we can all work more diligently toward achieving our dreams in life!

Thank you, and best of luck! Remember, you have what it takes to be the best, so be the best!

DESCRIPTION

Manipulation is commonly seen as a negative term, but it doesn't have to be that way. At its root, to manipulate something merely means to adjust it to get different results. For example, you might manipulate your hand around a pencil to make it easier to draw, shade, or color something in.

In sales, manipulation is an essential tactic. You must know how to see the value you have to offer someone, and manipulate them to see the value, too. Often, people will be quick to say "no" to something, even if it is something that can genuinely fulfill a need in their lives. It is your job to show them that need, how much better their lives could be with your offer, and why it is essential that they say "yes."

In *Mind Manipulation for Beginners,* we discuss the ethical approach to manipulation, enabling you to get past objectives and fulfill your needs, while also fulfilling others. Every tactic you discover in this book emphasizes the importance of a win-win approach, ensuring that you are always serving the best interest of your clients while meeting your objectives, as well. If that isn't enough, we also discuss how you can apply these ethical tactics to everyday situations, so you can get what you want, when you want it, just like a real boss!

Some of the specific manipulation strategies we discuss in *Mind Manipulation for Beginners* includes:

- What mind manipulation is and how to take an ethical approach
- The importance of influencing, rather than being influenced
- How your body language can manipulate someone else's thoughts
- The value of rapport and why you need to build trust and authority
- The snowball effect and how this technique will get you to "yes"
- Why the experience you offer matters, and how to make it good
- The importance of giving and why you should always give more than you take
- How to find the right timing and right opportunity so they can't say no
- The value of your mind power and how to expand that to expand your success
- How to apply these real-life techniques to everyday sales and circumstances
- An essential perspective you must have if you want to succeed in manipulation
- And more!

Manipulation can be done in an entirely ethical manner, and it can assist you in getting everything you desire in life. One of the most important concepts we discuss in *Mind Manipulation for Beginners* is the value of your desires, why you deserve to fulfill them, and why people want to help you fulfill these desires. When you discover this, you realize that sales have nothing to do with selling, and everything to do with serving to meet mutual needs.

If you are ready to up your skill and step into the world of mind manipulation, purchase *Mind Manipulation for Beginners* today and discover how you can apply these excellent tactics to your own approach! You will be so grateful that you did! Don't wait, get started now.

HOW TO ANALYZE PEOPLE

Learn How to Read People by Analyzing Body Language, Behavioral Psychology and Emotional Intelligence

Jenifer Thompson

© Copyright 2020 by Jenifer Thompson. All right reserved.

The work contained herein has been produced with the intent to provide relevant knowledge and information on the topic on the topic described in the title for entertainment purposes only. While the author has gone to every extent to furnish up to date and true information, no claims can be made as to its accuracy or validity as the author has made no claims to be an expert on this topic. Notwithstanding, the reader is asked to do their own research and consult any subject matter experts they deem necessary to ensure the quality and accuracy of the material presented herein.

This statement is legally binding as deemed by the Committee of Publishers Association and the American Bar Association for the territory of the United States. Other jurisdictions may apply their own legal statutes. Any reproduction, transmission, or copying of this material contained in this work without the express written consent of the copyright holder shall be deemed as a copyright violation as per the current legislation in force on the date of publishing and the subsequent time thereafter. All additional works derived from this material may be claimed by the holder of this copyright.

The data, depictions, events, descriptions and all other information forthwith are considered to be true, fair, and accurate unless the work is expressly described as a work of fiction. Regardless of the nature of this work, the Publisher is exempt from any responsibility of actions taken by the reader in conjunction with this work. The Publisher acknowledges that the reader acts of their own accord and releases the author and Publisher of any responsibility for the observance of tips, advice, counsel, strategies, and techniques that may be offered in this volume.

INTRODUCTION

Analyzing people is a behavior we all engage in, whether we realize it or not. In the animal kingdom, which we are all a part of, physical language is as important as verbal language. We pay attention to people's postures, body language, facial expressions, tones, and other non-verbal cues as a way to gain necessary information from people. The information we gain determines our "gut feeling" about a person, whether positive or negative and precisely what it means. Your instinct uses this as a way to determine the threats in your environment by identifying whether the threat comes from the environment itself, someone or something else, or if no threat exists at all.

Despite the fact that your primal brain is an expert with human analysis, your conscious mind may not be. In our modern lives, we have learned to ignore our instincts and follow our logic, which may not always be conditioned to pick up on the right information. For some people, their logical minds are conditioned to ignore others as a way to keep themselves comfortable and at peace in any situation.

Discovering how to analyze people consciously and intentionally is an excellent way to tap into the natural abilities of your primal brain and use them to your advantage. This analysis can allow you to determine your level of safety in an environment and help you determine how to best interact with other people. For example, you may be able to quickly identify that someone is outgoing and likes to communicate in an energized way. They may be more introverted and prefer to communicate in a more laid back manner. Knowing precisely how to engage with each person can deepen the quality of your friendships, expand your social circle, maximize your level of knowledge, and assist you with reaching your desired outcomes in any given circumstance. For example, if you are a salesperson, effective analysis can help you make better sales, or if you are a psychologist, effective analysis can help you gain deeper insight into a person's real troubles.

There are many points at which knowing how to analyze a person would be beneficial, and we are going to uncover them all and how to do it in this book. If you are ready to discover the unique skill of analyzing people, let's begin!

CHAPTER 1
Why Analyze People?

Analyzing people has many values, all of which lead to you getting what you desire out of any given situation. For example, the FBI uses analysis as a way to identify who is most likely to be guilty about something, who is lying, or who is innocent. Knowing how to adequately read people means you gain greater information from a person and a circumstance and that you can use that information to your advantage.

Another benefit of analyzing people is that it connects you with a more realistic insight into the human condition. People who do not consciously analyze other people may miss important social cues, leave themselves at risk of misunderstandings or miscommunications, or even put themselves in harmful situations due to an inability to adequately read the situation. It is important to know how to leverage this necessary primal ability so you can rely on it to support you in a number of ways, ranging from protecting you to helping you meet your desires. You will likely find your own unique reasons behind why you should learn how to analyze people. However, there are generally four core reasons behind why people analyze others': for business, social interaction, solutions, or confidence.

Analyzing People For Business

Analyzing people in business has been a necessary component of branding and marketing since the industry began. An effective analysis enables marketing experts to clearly understand the needs of their audience and meet those needs through branding and marketing initiatives. This is how they are able to design brands that match the exact desires of their audience while also creating marketing strategies that persuade their audience to interact with their brand.

Aside from creating aligned brands and marketing strategies, analysis has also enabled industries to unlock hidden growth opportunities so they can expand their businesses and industry growth. This type of analysis is often achieved by analyzing many individuals to create a large-scale analysis that represents a number of different people. In this case, they are analyzing for the majority to see what people are most interested in.

Salespeople also use analysis as a way to identify who is most likely to make a purchase and to decide how to sell to that individual. They will analyze for cues that indicate what a person cares about and what they need, then they use that to decide what to say and how to guide the experience. When they are effective, they create the exact experience their client needed to make a purchase, and they end up with a successful sale under their belts.

In business, an analysis may also be used as a way to determine which business moves a company or corporation might make. Individuals in a position of leadership or negotiation might use analysis to identify the intentions of another as they decide whether to make a business deal with that person or not. This way, they can be confident that they are making deals with honest people and getting their desires fulfilled from that deal.

Analyzing People For Social Interaction

Many people use analysis as a way to improve their social interactions. The original purpose of analysis in our primal instincts was for us to be able to determine whether someone else was a threat or not. We also used it as a way to generally analyze the tribe we were running with so that if one showed signs of distress or impending danger, the rest could be on alert and protect themselves from whatever may be threatening them. These days, the same is still useful; however, being able to analyze people can get you a lot further than threat analysis, too.

Analyzing people effectively can be a great way to make friends, grow your network, and enjoy healthier social interactions with others. When you know what to look for and how to read body language and nonverbal cues, you can quickly identify the best people to associate yourself with and the best way to engage with that individual. For example, let's say you are at a networking event, and you walk into a room filled with people that are all mingling. Through analysis, you could quickly identify the archetypes of everyone in the room so that you did not waste any time approaching people with the wrong archetype for your network. Once you identified the ones with the right archetype, you could quickly discover necessary information about how to communicate with them based on their nonverbal interactions with the room around them. From there, you could engage in a way that rapidly built your rapport, established a connection, and effectively added that person to your network.

This type of analysis is excellent for making new friends, dating new people, or just becoming better at socializing overall. Since socialization is necessary to so many areas of our lives and adds deeply to the value of our human experiences, it is well worth it to learn how to analyze people so you can enjoy improved connections with others.

Analyzing People For Solutions

Many times in life, you will be required to look for solutions to a circumstance you face. Salespeople are tasked with looking for solutions on a regular basis, as they must find solutions to meet the needs of their clients. Every day people are tasked with finding solutions to a variety of conflicts they might face, many involving other people that also need to be on board with that solution for it to work.

Analyzing people for solutions requires you to rapidly gain insight into their mood, their perspective toward the conflict, and their need. All of this can be gained by analyzing their verbal and nonverbal cues to get to the root of their concerns, at which point you can use this knowledge to propose a solution that is likely to fit that person's needs. The value of being in the position of creating and offering solutions is that you get to choose solutions that fit your needs, as well as the needs of the other person. This is an empowering position to be in, as people begin to trust in you and look toward you as the leader of that situation, which expands your reputation and the type of interactions you have with other people.

Analyzing People To Deepen Your Confidence

As social creatures, it makes sense that we thrive most when we are engaged in healthy, meaningful interactions with other people. From relationships to quick conversations at the checkout line, we value having positive interactions with others. These interactions deepen our sense of belonging, fulfillment, and satisfaction as we realize that we are accepted by others, which is a basic human need. People that learn to ignore their instinct about other people, or that have an intellectual disability that renders this instinct damaged, often lack confidence around others'. Their inability to clearly understand another often leads to them engaging in negative experiences because they cannot adequately read the situation and adjust their behavior accordingly.

Learning how to analyze people and use that analysis to make meaningful decisions about how to interact with another individual enables a person to develop greater confidence in themselves, especially when other people are concerned. Rather than feeling insecure or fearful of their interactions with others, they develop confidence in their ability to enjoy positive interactions. This increases their ability to feel as though they belong, which creates a sense of fulfillment and satisfaction on a deep, primal level.

CHAPTER 2
Get To Know Body Language

The biggest task you can tackle when it comes to discovering how to analyze other people is to learn to read body language. Much like animals in the wild communicate through their posture and movements, humans also communicate in this way. Although we rarely discuss body language as a part of everyday learning experiences, we all learn lessons of body language simply through observing others'.

Body language varies from person to person and can also have drastic differences across different cultures and groups of people. However, one can always rapidly pick up on the true intentions of another person simply through reading their body language, whether they come from the same place or not. Reading body language effectively comes partially through relying on your instinct and partially through researching the meaning of different bodily postures and cues for clearer understanding. Fortunately, psychologists and behavioral researchers have been looking into body language for years and have uncovered impressive amounts of knowledge around what the different cues mean and how they can be read.

The best way to begin reading body language is to go to a public place and start looking at different individuals. Observe their posture, physical movements, and behaviors to discover what each person is likely thinking, feeling, or doing. You will rapidly notice patterns that categorize people into different archetypes, which you can then read based on the different signs of body language below. The more you observe others' and understand what their body language means, the better you will be at reading body language as a way to analyze people.

Pay Attention To Proximity

Proximity references the amount of space between yourself and another person. When someone stands or sits close to another person, they feel a sense of closeness with that individual, which is why they have closed the space between them. If someone backs up or moves away, however, this means they are feeling uncomfortable, and they want to create more space between themselves and the other person. When a person is especially close to another individual, to the point where they are physically touching or are about to be physically touching, this indicates that they want to be physically close with that individual. This is commonly seen between romantic partners or partners that share some level of physical connection with each other.

Keep in mind that, in some cultures, it is customary to respect people's personal space, so they tend to leave more distance between themselves and others. In this case, it is helpful to pay attention to how they interact with all people and to observe their other body language indicators.

Beware Of Mirrored Behaviors

To mirror someone's behavior means to essentially mimic their behaviors. For example, if you were to stroke your hair and immediately after the person you are talking to touched their hair, this would be a sign of mimicked behaviors. Mimicked behaviors can range from posture to how you physically carry yourself or the actions you are taking, so pay close attention to how someone is mirroring someone else's behaviors. Suppose they are mirroring a lot of the behaviors. In that case, it means they are engaged with the other person and are generally interested in them. If they are not mirroring a lot of the other person's behaviors, it means they are disengaged or disinterested in that person. Be patient, though, as it can take as many as 10-30 seconds for the behavior to be mirrored by the other individual.

Look For Head Movements

Head movement can indicate a lot, such as the level of patience someone has with you or the person they are communicating with. For example, someone that nods their head slowly is interested in what you have to say and hopes you will continue talking. On the other hand, someone rapidly nodding their head means they are done listening, and they want you to stop talking so they can leave the conversation.

Aside from nodding, head tilting can indicate a lot about someone's level of interest, too. If someone tilts their head sideways while talking to another individual, this means they are interested in what the other person has to say, and they want to know more. If they tilt their head back, they are skeptical or uncertain about what the other person is saying, while tilting their head forward means they are interested or have an affinity with the speaker.

Another thing to pay attention to is the amount someone is being looked at, especially by the others around them. A person that is important and has a great rapport with others' will be looked at often, while someone who lacks significance will not be looked at by other people nearly as much. If you are looking to speak to the most powerful person in the room, look for the person that is being looked at the most.

Draw A Line From Their Toes

The direction a person's foot is facing says a lot about what they are interested in and where they truly want to be. If you are trying to analyze someone who is likely monitoring their body language and purposefully manipulating it to convey certain messages, the best thing you can do is look at their feet. Usually, people become so focused on adjusting their upper body language and facial expressions that they forget to pay attention to where their feet are directed. Their feet' direction tells you what they are interested in and what they would like to be doing at any given moment.

If a person's feet are pointed in your direction, this means that they have a favorable opinion of you and that they are interested in you. If their feet are pointed in another direction, this indicates something else. For example, feet pointed toward the door indicate someone is ready to leave, while feet pointed toward the bathroom might indicate someone needs to relieve themselves.

The next time you are in a group setting, pay attention to the directions of everyone's feet. You will quickly find out who likes who and if they are genuinely engaged with another person or not. You will also recognize who wants to leave, who would rather be elsewhere, and who is interested in continuing conversations with the person they are chatting up.

Observe Their Hand Signals

Hands also leak important information about what a person is thinking or feeling, so pay close attention to their hands and hand signals. When a person puts their hands in their pocket or on their head, this means they are either nervous or trying to deceive someone else in the room, though it can also indicate that they are relaxed depending on the rest of their body language. If their body is tense, tight, or closed off in any way, hands in the pocket indicate nervousness, while a person that is relaxed, standing with their legs apart, and seems casual, is indicating that they are comfortable in the moment.

The direction people point in or where their hands are closest to also indicates important information about that person. People will often point toward a person they have an affinity with and keep their hands generally closer to that person when they are communicating. They may not constantly point; however, you will notice they have more gestures going toward that person over anyone else, which is what indicates their level of interest.

If someone is supporting their head with their elbows on the table, this indicates they are bored. Boredom can also be witnessed in a person that stares at their hands or fidgets excessively with their hands while staring off into space. On the other hand, if they are fidgeting with their hands while rapidly looking around the room or holding a tense posture, this means they are feeling uncomfortable or nervous and are trying to relieve themselves of that energy.

Examine Their Arms

A person's arms are often considered the doorway to a person's self, as they can be used to block off the body or open it up to others. If a person stands with their arms crossed while looking at you, this typically means they are feeling defensive or intimidated by your presence. This may also indicate they are feeling vulnerable or anxious, so they want to be removed from the present moment. Alternatively, some people will cross their arms while maintaining a relaxed posture and a genuine smile, which means they are feeling relaxed and confident, though they may be trying to block off a certain aspect of themselves at that moment.

If someone places their hands on their hips, this is typically a display of dominance. Men are more likely to hold this posture than women, though women will often do it when they want to assert themselves. Some psychologists have recommended holding your hands on your hips and looking in the mirror at yourself in this posture for 60 seconds as a way to increase your self-confidence in any given moment because you see yourself holding a dominant posture. This pose indicates a deep sense of confidence and power, so you can assume anyone holding this posture feels dominant at that moment.

CHAPTER 3
Facial Expressions Speak Volumes

Facial expressions are similar to body language, except they are more subtle and fleeting than body language. Often, postures or gestures are held for at least a few seconds before changing, though they will typically last several minutes. Alternatively, facial expressions can be over within seconds, or sometimes even milliseconds, so you have to be paying close attention to catch these. Another thing about facial expressions is that you need to learn how to scan people's faces without coming across as though you are staring at them, as staring at people will completely change their mood, effectively changing their behaviors, too.

One benefit of reading facial expressions is that they tend to communicate more than the body does. While people have an easy time manipulating their body language, it can be far more challenging to monitor your facial expressions, so they do not "give you away." More often than not, people cannot control their fleeting facial expressions, which means you can rapidly gain a deeper understanding of what they think and feel, especially about particular subjects in conversation.

In general, there are seven micro expressions you can look for in a person's face, which are the fleeting expressions that indicate how they really feel. If a person is trying to save face or provide specific energy to a situation, they may try to hide these expressions in an effort to avoid having you find out what they really think or feel. Fortunately, these micro expressions happen regardless of how hard someone tries to avoid it, so if you watch for them, you will certainly see them.

Expressions Of Surprise

Expressions of surprise can be seen in a person raising their eyebrows to the point where they curve, and the skin below the eyebrow stretches out. You will also see horizontal wrinkles across the forehead, as their brows press up far enough to allow their eyelids to open more than is typical, too. Often, a person that is surprised will have their jaw drop open, and their teeth will be parted, though there should be no tension or stretching of the mouth itself. In the dating world, when someone gives you a fleeting look of surprise, this is said to be a good sign that they are attracted to you, interested in you, and that they want to spend more time with you.

Expressions Of Fear

Fear can be seen in the eyebrows as well, as they will be raised though they will also be drawn together, creating a flat line across the brows. You will see wrinkles on the forehead, but they are at the center of it between the person's eyebrows only. Often, their upper eyelid will be raised, but the lower eyelid will be drawn up as it has become tenser. Often, you will see a lot of white above the iris of the eye, but no white below the iris, because of how far the eyes are drawn up. In the mouth area, their mouth will be open with their lips slightly tensed or stretched. Some people may also draw their lips back, making a dimple in the sides of their mouths.

Expressions Of Disgust

Disgust can be seen in the face whenever a person narrows their eyes, raises their upper lip and cheeks, and wrinkles their nose. In some cases, their upper lip may be raised so high that you can see their upper teeth, too. Disgust is not only a reaction to seeing or smelling something gross; it can also be toward something a person hears about. For example, if you are out with a new friend and you say something they are disgusted by, such as mentioning a food you like that they don't, you might see this expression on their face.

Expressions Of Anger

Anger is often easy to witness in someone's face, though some people will attempt to hide their anger, which means you need to pay close attention to their faces. When a person is angry, their eyebrows will be lowered and drawn together, creating vertical lines at the center of their forehead, between their eyebrows. Their lower lip will be tensed in a pout-like position, and their lips may be firmly pressed together with the corners of the mouth drawn down and their lower jaw jutting out. Often, their eyes will be glaring or even bulging because they are so angry. You might also notice that their nostrils are flaring.

Expressions Of Happiness

When a person is happy, their face looks soft and drawn back. Even if they are not smiling, the corners of their mouth are often drawn back and up, and they may even have their mouth parted with their teeth exposed. Often, a wrinkle will run from the outer nostril to the outer corner of the lip, indicating they are feeling happy. When a person smiles, even subtly, their cheeks will be raised, and their lower eyelid might have small wrinkles or tension. Crow's feet near the outside of the eyes also indicates that a person is feeling happy at that moment. The more defined the various wrinkles and lines of happiness are, the happier someone is feeling.

Expressions Of Sadness

When a person is sad, the inner corners of their eyebrows will be drawn in and up, creating either a flat brow or a brow that arches down toward the edges of the face. Below their eyebrows, the skin may be triangulated with the inner corner up. Often, the corners of their lips will be drawn down, but their jaw will be drawn up. Their lower lip will also pout, though it may be subtle in some people, especially if they are trying to hide their sadness from others.

Expressions Of Contempt Or Hate

The only way to really recognize a look of contempt or hate is to look for someone that has one side of the mouth raised, despite the rest of the face being neutral or natural. Contempt and hate indicate someone is feeling negative toward another individual or something that an individual is saying. This is the only microexpression that is asymmetrical, as all of the other ones are symmetrical in nature.

CHAPTER 4
The Fbi's Method For Eye Analysis

Studies have shown that eye movement indicates what is going on in someone's brain, and therefore what they are likely feeling or thinking in any given moment. Paying close attention to someone's eye movement allows you to recognize whether they are truthful or not at any given moment. The most important things to notice are where a person is looking and what they are specifically doing with their eyes. Generally, the eyes are used as a way to identify dishonesty in someone, as there are common indicators people use that express their dishonesty through their eyes. However, if you do not see these indicators, chances are you are talking to a person that is telling you the truth.

Pay Attention To Where Their Eyes Go

Where someone spends most of their time looking reveals a lot about what they are thinking or feeling. When a person frequently looks at you and pays close attention to what you are doing, this indicates that they are interested in you and want to know more about you. If a person looks excessively at someone else, this means they are more interested in that individual, and they want to know more about them. A person who stares heavily at a specific object or place is revealing what they would rather be doing. For example, if a person stares heavily toward the door, they want to leave, while a person that stares heavily toward a television would rather be watching TV than doing whatever they are presently doing. People look at what they are interested in or at the person or object that has their attention most.

Eye Signals Of Lying

If a person is lying, their eyes will move up and to the right because they are attempting to make something up on the spot or recall the lie they made up previously. If, however, a person looks up and to the left, they are likely telling the truth because the way they are looking indicates they are trying to remember a real piece of information. If someone is looking around, it may not necessarily mean they are lying, though. Some people will move their eyes a lot to process information, which is an entirely different movement.

Eye Signals Of Stress

If someone is feeling stressed, you will see it through increased blinking. The average person blinks between 8 to 21 times per minute, so if someone is blinking excessively, such as once every two or three seconds, this means they are stressed out by the present moment. They may be stressed overall, or they may be feeling pressured to answer a question properly, which introduces temporary stress to their system.

Eye Signals Of Disgust / Distaste

When someone feels disgusted with something, they will often narrow their eyes. The more narrow someone's eyes are, the more disgusted they are feeling at that moment, so be aware of *how* narrow their eyes are to better understand how they are feeling.

Eye Signals Of Discomfort

When someone is uncomfortable, they will do something called "eye blocking." Eye blocking means they are trying to cover their eyes to avoid you seeing them. If they cannot reasonably block their eyes, they may avoid eye contact altogether in an effort to avoid having to make eye contact when they are uncomfortable.

Eye Signals Of Happiness

When a person is feeling happy, their eyes may do many things. Often, they will arch their eyebrows and smile. They will also have enlarged pupils, which is a sign that you like something. In fact, studies have shown that if you look at someone or something you love, your pupil size will automatically increase, indicating your affection. Of course, this may not be easy to witness in other people, but you might be able to see it if you pay close enough attention.

Eye Signals Of Fear Or Surprise

If a person is feeling fearful or surprised, their eyes will often be wide open. They might also have a fleeting look of surprise where their eyes go from wide to wider and back to wide, indicating that they are especially surprised by something. This is an automatic response caused by adrenaline in the body, which you can witness in someone else if you pay close enough attention.

Eye Signals Of Focus

When someone is especially focused, their pupils will usually constrict, and their eyes will remain fixated on what has their focus. However, if they are focused on something that is in the distance, their pupils will actually dilate instead.

CHAPTER 5
Trust Your Intuition

Your intuition, or instinct, knows more than you think. This inner compass is fixed to the primal part of your brain, and it knows how to pick up information from a situation that your conscious self may not have picked up on otherwise. While we are often conditioned to ignore this part of ourselves, we can learn to regain a connection with it by trusting our intuition and using it regularly.

Psychologists and researchers believe our intuitions and instincts are so powerful because they are reading information that our conscious mind does not have time for. In one second, you process more than 11,000,000 pieces of information. Naturally, your conscious mind does not have time to sort through all of that information to decipher what it all means, so it focuses instead on what is relevant to you at that moment. In other words, it fixates on what you have chosen to bring into your conscious awareness. Just because you are not consciously thinking about all of these things does not mean they cease to exist, however. Your brain is still taking in all of this information, and your subconscious mind is still sorting through it all to better understand what it all means. If it finds something of importance, it raises it up through your awareness of the necessary level of consciousness. If it does not feel the need to raise it to your conscious awareness or does not have a complete set of information to raise to your conscious awareness, it will feed it into your intuition or instinct instead. Thus, you get those "gut feelings" about different circumstances, places, things, and *people*.

Don't Overthink Your Intuition

Your intuition is said to be a fast judge of character, and it is often more accurate than your logical mind, too. However, if you overthink your intuition or any of the information you have perceived through your intuition, you will disrupt your results and find yourself experiencing inaccuracies. The best way to analyze a person with your intuition is to trust the first gut feeling you get about them, or the feeling you get based on their first impression.

If you are observing someone to better understand their body language, facial expressions, tone, or even the meaning of their words, pay close attention to the initial reaction you have to whatever they have said. You will immediately pick up on whether or not they are trustworthy, what emotions are behind their words, and what thoughts they likely have that drive their emotion.

Avoid Attaching To Intuitive Beliefs

Intuition can provide you an excellent insight into a given situation; however, it is not helpful to attach yourself to your intuitive beliefs, especially if new information is presented. For example, if you believe someone wants to do something with you based on your intuition, but they verbally express that they do not want to, it is unhelpful to attach to the belief that they do want to and that they must be lying if they said otherwise. Attaching to beliefs is unhealthy, can remove you from reality, and can lead to uncomfortable or unfair situations between yourself and another individual.

One way that people tend to rapidly attach to their intuitive beliefs is through their dreams. When a person dreams of something, they can attach to the idea that their dreams are true and might refuse to believe anything that states otherwise. For example, if a person was planning on going on vacation but dreams about a plane crash, they might cancel the vacation or experience excess stress on the plane because of their dream. In this case, they have attached to the idea that their dream was real, and their intuition was warning them against the vacation, despite the fact that this was not something rooted in logic, reasoning, or facts.

Another way people tend to do this with others is by believing in something completely untrue and then developing anxiety over it. For example, you might have an intuitive feeling that someone is harshly judging you, and that feeling causes you to feel anxious and scared. You might even try to change yourself or twist yourself to conform to their beliefs because you want them to change their opinion. If, however, they are not actually harshly judging you and you have misinterpreted their signals, you are wasting your time and maybe causing an uncomfortable social experience in the process. It helps to listen to your intuition *and* trust that people will tell you the truth about what they are thinking and feeling. Even if they are not, it is not your responsibility to force someone to express their genuine judgments. Respect their right to stay quiet, and focus on yourself.

Practice Improves Your Intuition

Like anything, your intuition can be improved upon with practice. To improve your intuition, you simply need to listen to it more and trust the feelings it gives you. For example, if you are in a room and your intuition tells you that the room is dangerous or that you should leave it, trust it and leave that space. You might not understand why, and the reasoning may never be revealed to you, but so long as you trust your intuition, you are reinforcing it and encouraging it to continue supporting your wellbeing.

Another way you can improve your intuition, which can directly help you analyze people, is through quieting your mind and giving your intuition space to work. If you are continually thinking back through everything you logically and reasonably know, you will be dominating your mind with thoughts that drown your intuition out. Try clearing your mind, observing another person, and inviting your intuition to provide you with feedback on that other individual. Then, read that feedback to get a clearer understanding of what your intuition is telling you.

Insight Is Seeing, Intuition Is Sensing

It is important to recognize that your insight and intuition are two separate things. Insight suggests you have actually seen something, such as the way a person is behaving or knowledge that allows you to better understand the way a person is behaving. Intuition, on the other hand, allows you to sense what another person is thinking or feeling. You might be able to sense information behind their behaviors, or that indicate why they are engaging in specific behaviors. However, intuition is only a feeling or a gut reaction; it is not a guarantee.

In order to effectively use your intuition in things such as analyzing people, it is helpful to allow your intuition to draw you to a conclusion, then use your logic and reasoning to determine whether your conclusion is accurate or not. If your insight suggests you misinterpreted that person, you might use your intuition to gain further knowledge based on what you learned through insight, but you should never assume that your insight is wrong. Always trust your intuition to guide you, but be willing to look for more information to guarantee your findings.

Stress Favors Intuition

When you are in a stressful situation, your intuition will tell you everything you need to know to navigate that experience. Intuition is spectacular at helping you move through troubling experiences effectively, so you remain safe throughout that experience. If you are in a situation where you are stressed out, and your intuition starts telling you something about the people around you, you can generally trust your intuition to be a fairly good judge of character.

However, if you are feeling sad, your intuition is not nearly as strong. When you are sad, your intuition is likely to be drowned out by a voice in your head that makes you feel worse. That voice will attempt to convince you that it is your intuition, but it isn't. As it attempts to convince you, it will also try to tell you that everything is bad, things are going wrong, no one likes you, and there is no hope for you. You can tell this is not your intuition because it speaks messages of hopelessness and defeat, rather than clear signals of how to get yourself out of that situation.

Be careful not to rely on your intuition when you are feeling sad or depressed, as doing so could lead to you trusting false information and struggling to truly read the other person. Instead, rely on more practical measures such as reading their body language, facial expressions, and eyes.

You Can Read People Through Their Writing

One fascinating way that you can read people through your intuition is by reading them through their writing. In this day and age, everyone is on social media writing about what they are doing, how they are feeling, or what they are thinking about. Fascinatingly, you can read what someone has written and gained insight into who they are and what they are experiencing based on their words. Similarly to witnessing darting eyes, a tense brow, pressed lips or raised cheeks, you can read someone based on the words they use, their punctuation and grammar, and the general tone of their messages.

When a person writes emails, social media posts, streams of consciousness, blog posts, or anything else online, they are using cues that indicate who they are and what they are communicating. An excellent cue to look for would be the language they are using. People that swear, especially frequently, communicate that they are likely highly neurotic, lack conscientiousness, and are unlikely to be agreeable with others. If they use any words that suggest anger, the same can generally be assumed. When a person speaks in the past tense, this is likely to indicate that they are depressed, while words like "know" in a diary suggest that they are feeling depressed, also.

Another way you can judge someone's character online is by looking at their profile. What username are they using? What is their profile picture? How have they described themselves in their bio? You can tell if someone is fun, whimsical, professional, angry, judgmental, self-centered, flamboyant, incompetent, or friendly based on how they have designed their profile and what words they have chosen to use.

A great way to practice using your intuition to help you identify someone's character is to look at people's social media profiles. Spend time analyzing profiles to get a feel for what type of personality someone has. Scan over their entire profile and trust your intuition to guide you to the right conclusion on who that person likely is. Then, if possible, scroll their posts and see if they align with the assumption you have drawn.

CHAPTER 6
Become Aware Of Emotional Energy

Emotional energy is a form of energy that we all carry, and it is expressed through our verbal and nonverbal cues. Everyone can sense and experience emotional energy because it is a commonly used form of communication that allows humans to share important information with each other. From person to person, emotional communication can help people connect or ward off the other person. In groups, emotional communication can help the rest of the group become aware of a problem or increase their feelings of comfort and relaxation, depending on what is going on.

Like with all other forms of analysis, you can read energy through your intuition. However, there are other ways to read emotional energy, too. Learning how to read emotional energy practically ensures that you will have the ability to rely on your intuition and your knowledge to effectively read a person. This way, you gain more accurate reading, and you can use that knowledge to your benefit.

Sense People's Presence

People emit energy when they are present in a space, and that energy can be felt by everyone else. An excellent way to recognize this fact is to consider the last time a friend visited your house; you could feel their energy in your home. It is easy to sense someone else's energy in your home because this is a place where you spend a lot of time, so when the energy changes, it is noticeable. Another excellent way to sense people's presence is to think about the different energies between someone, such as the Dalai Lama versus Charles Manson.

Everyone, including yourself, exudes certain energy when they are present, and it pays to identify what that energy is anytime you meet someone new. Pay close attention to the overall energy people emit and the way it makes you feel. Notice when they feel warm, positive, and enjoyable to be around, or when they feel cold, detached, or draining to be around. These all indicate specific energy archetypes that the person is likely to have.

Pay Attention To Their Eyes

The age-old saying "Eyes are the window to a person's soul" is true. You can express love, hate, and many other powerful emotions through your eyes. Science has shown that your brain emits electromagnetic signals through the eyes that can be sensed by other people, and vice versa. You can sense this energy anytime you feel someone staring at you, even if you were not originally looking at that person.

If you want to know what emotions a person is feeling, look into their eyes, and pay close attention to the types of looks they give back. Trust your intuition, but be aware of other tell-tale signs, too. If they refuse to look at you, they may be uncomfortable or angry with you or with something else that is causing them to feel disconnected from others'. If they look deep into your eyes and you feel seen, received, and loved, you know they have an energy of compassion and empathy. If you feel hated, uncomfortable, or like you are being hunted, you are in the presence of someone that does not have your best interest at heart. Your intuition will tell you the true meaning behind someone's glance, so trust that and incorporate it into your overall analysis to get a clear image of how a person is feeling and what they are thinking.

Feel Their Physical Touches

A person's physical touches heavily communicate the way they are feeling. The primary points of touch include handshakes, hugging, random touching, and welcomed touching. Each of these touch-based experiences can communicate significant amounts of energy to you, so pay attention.

Handshakes are a form of touch that you can experience with anyone, and you can initiate with anyone at appropriate times, too. You can gain a significant amount of information from a handshake, as this simple form of touch can tell you if a person is feeling weak or confident, engaged or disinterested, outgoing or withdrawn. How a person's body language is surrounding that handshake says a lot, too. If a person leans toward you, is fully facing you, looks at you, or has their feet pointed toward you, they are engaged and feeling good about your conversation. If they are neutral or holding themselves back in any way, they are not interested in communicating at that moment.

Hugs can say a lot, too. If a person hugs you from the side or pats your back during a hug, this indicates they feel friendly toward you but not as though you are super close. The pat indicates the person is feeling uneasy, and while they care about you, they are uncertain as to what the appropriate form of expression is to convey that. If a person hugs you from behind, this means they see you as a lover; it is only ever shared between lovers, too. Hugs from behind indicate a person feels protective over you, and they want to show you how much they cherish you through this hug. When a person offers you a tight hug, especially when that hug turns into an embrace, it means they are letting you know they care. A-frame hugs are hugs where a person hugs you out of obligation, not desire, so they keep most of their body away from you except for their shoulders.

Random acts of touching are acts that are not necessary nor expected, but they do happen. For example, if someone touches your shoulder, arm, or leg when you are talking to them. Touching is almost never accidental, as we tend to be highly aware of who we are around and will avoid touching or physically connecting with someone if we truly do not want to. If someone is making contact with you, it is because they want to. This virtually always signals that the person is interested in you and engaged at that moment. In some cases, these touches indicate a person cares or is connecting with you to help you feel better. If it seems random to you, however, it is likely that they are communicating interest in you.

Intentional acts of touching are most common among lovers, and they can say a lot. Since you likely experience touch from your partner often, you can tell a change in their emotions based on a change in their touch. Less touching, lighter touching, or seemingly restrictive touching indicates that a person is feeling disconnected or like they do not actually want to be in physical contact at that moment. If your partner does this, they may be feeling stressed out, having a hard day, or struggling with a sense of disconnect between the two of you. If your partner is touching you more than usual, this indicates they want to feel closer to you, so they are trying to get closer to your physical space. You can always ask them to communicate their thoughts, feelings, and needs if you require clarification on why they are behaving the way they are.

Listen To Their Tone And Laugh

You can immediately tell if someone is fake in their communication or laughter, based exclusively on their tones. A person with a tone and laugh that is genuine will come from a deep, centered place, and their voice and laughter will sound hearty and full. If they sound hollow, empty, or forced, they are faking it to cover up what they are really feeling or thinking.

You can also hear emotions such as anger, sadness, low confidence, anxiety, insensitivity, and arrogance in a person's voice. Simply through listening to their tone and the way they are enunciating their words, you can pick up on the different emotions in their voice. This particular form of hearing is best achieved by listening to many emotions, which allows you to genuinely hear the differences in emotion. Often, they are so subtle that attempting to explain them would be challenging. A great way to practice hearing emotional energy in a person's voice is to listen to videos or recordings with people that have many different emotions. See if you can identify each emotion as it surfaces, and then check to see if your assumption was correct. This way, you can start to pick up on hearing emotional energy in people's voices and laughs.

Sense Their Heart Energy

Each of us has heart energy that we can bring, or leave, from any experience. When a person brings their heart energy, you feel a sense of fullness around that person. They communicate and behave in ways that make it clear that they have shown up as their full selves and that they feel deeply invested in the present moment. If a person does not bring their heart energy, you can sense that, too, as they seem to be lacking a certain "something." Often, a person that is guarding their heart or purposefully leaving it out of a situation emanates an energy that is ineffable or difficult to describe. Something about them just feels "off" or "missing." If you know a person well, you will be able to quickly tell if their heart is not in it, while people you have just met may require more patience as you learn how to read their unique energy and expressions.

With some people, you can just tell that they are not fully invested in what they are doing or saying. With others, you need to pay closer attention. Can you feel their warmth, unconditional love, and positive intentions radiating as they move through life? Or does it seem like they are agitated, annoyed, or frustrated with the things they have been tasked with? People with big heart energy will always express some form of passion and peace, even if they are doing something they dislike because, at their core, they are a genuinely passionate and peaceful person. Those that completely lack these expressions during times of stress or disappointment are disconnected from their heart and may not be behaving or communicating authentically at that moment. If they are generally disconnected from their heart, they may not know how to behave or communicate authentically at all. In this case, you need to pay more attention to their expressions and nonverbal language so you can get a clearer interpretation of their real intentions and messages.

CHAPTER 7
Develop Your Baseline Understanding

Armed with the knowledge you have, you are ready to start analyzing people. It is not helpful, however, to go into the process with a variety of knowledge and no palpable way to apply that knowledge in the actual moment. When you are actively analyzing people, you do not have time to pause, read through your book, identify their behavior, and move on to the next one. Body language, facial expressions, eyes, and emotional energy are expressed and changed so rapidly that it would be impossible for you to read everything step by step. That is why, in effective human analysis, there is a process you can follow that allows you to effortlessly read someone, gain accurate feedback, and move on to the next portion of your reading. This process starts with creating your baseline analysis. A baseline analysis will vary depending on the situation you are in. With people that you know well or are around frequently, you have many encounters to generate baseline data, so you know how they generally behave. For people that you will only see once or twice, you do not have nearly as much time to put together an understanding of how that person generally behaves or what their overall baseline is. Instead, you will put one together that is relevant to your interaction and use that to define the rest of your analysis.

The Meaning Of A Baseline

A person's baseline is their typical behavior. This defines the average emotional state of an individual, as well as their typical thoughts, actions, perspectives, and their overall approach to life. Baselines can easily be summarized in a few words or less, which makes defining and tracking them easier.

The purpose of a baseline analysis is that it allows you to understand what their average behavior is like, which allows you to identify when they have deviated away from that baseline. For example, let's say your boss is generally a hard ruler. Perhaps he tends to deliver orders with a harsh tone, has high expectations, and is not afraid to ream someone out if they fail to meet those expectations fully. This would be your boss's baseline analysis. If one day, your boss came to work and was not doling out consequences, snapping orders at people, and ruling with a hard fist, you would know something was off.

Baselines are important because they help you understand how your actions, others' actions, or the circumstances are affecting a person. You may need to have this awareness so you can take actions that support someone, protect yourself, or resolve the conflict of a situation you might face. In some cases, baselines will be unimportant because your analysis will not require further action, but there will be many times in your life that you have to communicate with others, and using baselines is an excellent way to gauge your effectiveness.

Baselines In Long Term Relationships

In long term relationships, you have a significant number of opportunities to identify someone's baseline and build on it. People's long term baseline changes over time, so your general understanding of a person is likely to change over time, too. For example, your friend might have been a carefree, spontaneous type of person, then they had a child, and now they are more reserved and careful. These types of changes, especially in response to life experiences, are entirely normal. The benefit of knowing a person's long term baseline is that you can become aware of how they have changed, and you can learn a lot about them through those changes. You also discover how you can better interact with them based on these changes and continue to enjoy an excellent relationship with them.

The baseline in a long term relationship will start off the same as a baseline in a one-off encounter because when you first meet someone, you do not have any historical data to add to your baseline analysis. As you continue to get to know them, you gain significant insight into how they tend to think, feel, and behave in different situations, which allows you to build a more dynamic baseline.

The more you learn about a person and their baseline in different situations, the more you understand them. This understanding may be seemingly irrelevant, or it may help you connect with or support the people in your life better. For example, let's say you have a friend that is generally optimistic and outgoing in all areas of her life, but when it comes to her career, she seems more intimidated and shy and behaves completely differently. This lets you know that something in her career is causing her to feel a lack of confidence. You may or may not be in a position to support her; however, this awareness allows you to have greater compassion and empathy for the experiences she has in this part of her life.

You will come to discover people's baselines so long as they are a long-term fixture in your life, whether you intend to or not. For example, your family, friends, coworkers, and other people you see on a regular basis will all become people with whom you share long term relationships. Knowing the baselines of people in these long term relationships allows you to use this to your advantage anytime you need to, which can be a powerful position to hold at any given time in your life.

Baselines In One-Off Encounters

In one-off encounters, you do not have nearly as much time to create a baseline, which means you must accept that right from the start, your baseline analysis will be incomplete. With people such as the person that serves you coffee, a person you are selling something to, or a person on the bus, you do not have insight into how they tend to behave in their everyday life. You lack awareness around their baseline with their family, work, friends, hobbies, and in other key areas of their lives where they are likely to express their true baseline personality. The trouble with this is that you only have so much to go from, which means you only know their baseline at that moment. However, for most short term encounters, that is all you need.

Let's say you are working retail, and someone comes into your store angry because of an experience they had with the company you are working for. To you, their baseline is angry because this is the only way you have seen them. Although this is unlikely to be their overall baseline, it is the baseline you can analyze and use to help you assess how well or not your conversation is going. If, after talking with them, they deviate toward anger, you know your actions are not supporting their situation. If, however, they start to deviate toward more peaceful and cheerful, you know that your solution is fulfilling their need and they are satisfied with their experience.

In many one-off encounters, you will not directly engage with the person whose baseline you are reading. However, you may want to know their baseline so you can observe how they deviate from it in encounters with other people. This information may not be directly relevant to you, but it can help you gain a deeper understanding of how people tend to behave, what may affect their baseline, and what to look for when reading people. The more you practice reading people, even if you are not directly associated with that person, the better you will get at this skill.

Defining Someone's Baseline

The actual act of defining someone's baseline should be done immediately upon meeting someone, before ever trying to understand what their verbal or nonverbal communications mean about that specific moment. To identify someone's baseline, give yourself about 1-2 minutes to observe the way they carry themselves and make a conclusion from what you discover. You will create your baseline from their body language, facial expressions, eye movements, and overall energy.

Once you have established their baseline, give yourself another 3-5 minutes to confirm that your conclusion is correct, and to judge how flexible they are with their baseline. If they are particularly flexible, they will rapidly deviate away from your initial conclusion. If they are not, they will remain consistent in their baseline.

If someone's baseline is something you find pleasant or that you want to continue experiencing, pay close attention to the thing that causes their baseline to change and elect to encourage circumstances that maintain or improve their baseline. If you want their baseline to change, such as if they are in a low mood, beware of behaviors that change their circumstances, and engage only in those that improve the way they are feeling.

Anytime you are directly engaging with someone, you always want to pay attention to how your behavior affects their baseline and adjust your behavior to affect their baseline in a positive, not negative, way. It is important, however, not to use this as a way to fuel people-pleasing behaviors. Your goal is not to betray yourself or your needs to fulfill someone else's so that they are happy. Instead, you must remain consistent in having your needs fulfilled, though you can go about getting them fulfilled in a way that aligns with the other person, too. The real goal is to use their baseline and the behaviors that cause them to deviate as a way to understand how you can get your needs met through that person if the circumstances warrant it. Otherwise, this is merely for observational and educational purposes.

CHAPTER 8
Pay Close Attention To People Deviating Away

Deviations define the process of someone moving away from their baseline personality. Generally, deviations can be positive, negative, or neutral. When a person deviates away from their baseline, this indicates that something has caused them to feel different from their normal state. Every person deviates from their baseline, so this is entirely normal behavior. However, deviations can tell you a lot about a person overall, as well as in that present moment.

As you learn to analyze people, it is helpful to pay attention to when and where deviations occur, as well as what is causing them. In some cases, observing deviations will merely support your ability to create a deeper understanding of humans and their tendencies. In other cases, deviations allow you to understand how you or your environment is influencing someone and possibly provide you with opportunities to use that to your advantage.

It is important to realize that observing specific behaviors from people does not mean you are required to act on that information. For the most part, recognizing these behaviors will not require any effort on your behalf; it will merely serve as added data for you to monitor, which will assist you in future endeavors. When it does come time for you to act on that data, however, deviations serve as a key opportunity for you to determine the best course of action for you to take, should you have needs that require fulfillment.

People Routinely Deviate From Their Baseline

Firstly, you must understand that people routinely deviate from their baseline. When you are with people for an incredibly short period of time, you may witness only one or two deviations, or you may not witness any. As you spend more time with people, however, you will witness significant deviations from their baseline as people are constantly being affected by their environment, the people around them, and even the experiences they have within themselves.

Deviations from baselines may be spontaneous, or they may be habitual. Spontaneous deviations indicate a person is experiencing an unusual reaction to something which has drawn them away from their baseline. An excellent example would be if a person had recently experienced a tragedy such as a car accident or a sudden loss, which would cause a deviation. These types of deviations can be significant and can elicit unusual behavior from an individual. These unusual behaviors are generally more challenging to analyze and predict unless you are accustomed to analyzing people across many situations.

Habitual deviations are routinely experienced and generally occur on a daily, weekly, or monthly basis. They are common, to the point where even you experience these deviations on a regular basis. Habitual deviations are caused by triggers which a person is routinely exposed to, thus causing them to deviate from their baseline to fulfill that habitual experience. These deviations are triggered by common occurrences in one's life, such as career, family, friends, hobbies, specific songs or TV shows, or other experiences. For example, a person that is generally calm and friendly might become competitive and assertive when faced with their career because this persona suits their career better.

Habitual deviations are experienced in virtually every area of someone's life and can be defined as categorical baselines, or baselines that are relevant to each area of a person's life. If you were to observe someone's categorical baselines, you would quickly recognize that they had baselines specific to eight areas of their lives: health, wealth, career, relationships, love, hobbies, their relationship with themselves, and their faith. Each of these areas can cause a person to experience different feelings, thoughts, and behaviors. If you have people that are close to you in your life, you can likely reflect on them or observe them and immediately witness these changed baselines. Overall, however, the baselines should all work together to create that individuals' primary baseline, or the baseline that represents who they are as a whole individual.

Negative Deviations Indicate Something Is Wrong

Negative deviations are those that cause an individual to experience negative emotions or engage in negative behaviors. Often, their thoughts and perspectives will follow a pessimistic suit, too. If a person experiences negative deviations from their baseline, you can easily assume something is likely wrong in that person's world. Negative deviations themselves will not tell you what is wrong, but they will indicate that said person is experiencing frustrations or challenges in a key area of their life.

The four likely influences of negative deviations are self, environment, others, and circumstances. Each of these can cause a person to experience a negative mood, thoughts, feelings, or behaviors. You must analyze their other cues to identify which is the likely cause of their negative deviation.

If a person is experiencing a negative deviation caused by themselves, they are being challenged by self-limiting beliefs, low confidence or self-esteem, or thoughts that are causing them to feel bad about themselves. People commonly dig into negative memories that were recalled based on a recent trigger, which causes them to experience a negative deviation.

For example, if a person was routinely bullied about something as a child, anytime they faced that trigger as an adult, they may have a negative deviation because they recall these painful memories.

If a person experiences negative deviation because of their environment, they are struggling to thrive within that space. The triggers they experience are caused by the space around them, and they cause that person to feel as though they cannot be happy or content within that space. Some triggers may be fleeting, such as a messy kitchen or laundry on the floor, while others may be more persistent. For example, some people are triggered by their place of employment because it has caused so much stress for them.

If a person experiences negative deviation due to others, they have been negatively impacted by another individual in one way or another. This can happen following conflict, betrayal, disappointment, unfulfilled expectations, or other challenges one may face with another individual. These negative deviations may be relieved once the conflict has been resolved, or it may be relieved once the offending individual leaves that person's space.

If a person experiences negative deviations caused by their circumstances, they are likely to deviate away from their baseline in all areas of their lives. Circumstances like trauma, major conflict, unexpected life changes, or situations that cause failure to thrive can all negatively affect a person. When they experience these negative deviations, they are only healed once that person's circumstances improve. They are often capable of adjusting the circumstances themselves, though some take time to be fully adjusted.

Positive Deviations Indicate Someone Is Pleased

Positive deviations are those that cause an individual to experience something positive or pleasant in relation to their baseline. Even people that have a generally positive baseline can experience positive deviations as they move from happiness or gratitude to excitement or elation. When a person experiences a positive deviation, this means something excellent is happening in their world that is promoting this positive experience.

Like with negative deviations, positive deviations are caused by one's self, environment, others, or their circumstances. You must observe a person's overall cues to gain more insight into what has encouraged a positive mood. With positive deviations, these can be particularly helpful with building relationships or positively impacting someone's life as you gain insight into what enables them to have these positive deviations. For example, if you learn that your friend is especially excited by surprises, you can plan surprises for them as a way to promote a positive deviation from their baseline anytime you want to celebrate them or help them enjoy the most out of life.

Positive deviations stimulated by one's self are the most powerful form of positive deviations. A person that can stimulate this deviation on their own knows how to elevate themselves out of a low place, which means they can improve their wellbeing without the necessary assistance of anyone else. Their positive deviations can be caused by experiences they created for themselves, their thoughts, beliefs, or values.

Positive deviations stimulated by one's environment indicate that they feel in their element in that environment, which causes them to thrive. When a person thrives in a given environment, they are more likely to experience improved mood, greater resiliency, increased determination, and a significant will to achieve anything they set out to achieve. Often, they experience a boost to their self-confidence and self-esteem, too, which is excellent for one's well being.

Positive deviations caused by other people are a wonderful sign that someone is pleased by another person's presence. Positive deviations in social settings can be caused by surrounding ourselves with people we like or sharing pleasant experiences with people we enjoy. If you are engaged in analyzing a person, and you want to have a positive impact on that individual, sharing pleasant experiences with them is a wonderful way to have a better experience with that person.

Positive deviations caused by one's circumstances means that someone is likely celebrating something meaningful in their life. A new birth, a promotion, a scholarship, engagements, new opportunities, and other experiences can all stimulate one to experience a positive deviation from their baseline.

As with negative deviations, most positive deviations are short-lived, though they will have a significant impact on someone's wellbeing. Generally, people that experience more positive deviations will enjoy greater health, improved self-confidence and self-esteem, and more fulfillment from life because they experience positive things on a regular basis.

Behaviors, Circumstances, And Experiences Affect Deviations

Every baseline can be affected by behaviors, circumstances, and experiences. While each person is responsible for their own baseline, it is common for other people's behaviors, circumstances, and experiences to impact another's baseline, too. People that are generally more resilient, leadership-oriented, and persistent in life tend to have greater control over their baseline, which allows them to refrain from being affected unnecessarily by things in their lives. This does not mean that a person will not have negative or positive deviations; those are inevitable and are experienced by everyone. However, people with greater control will generally experience fewer deviations, or more intentional deviations, because they are less affected by the people around them.

It is important to recognize the level to which a person is affected by the world around them if you want to observe more about who they are and how they are influenced. People that are easily affected by external factors can be easy to manipulate and affect and can also be more flighty and lack commitment. You must be continually influencing this individual to remain on the same page as you if you are attempting to work with someone that is routinely affected by external influences; otherwise, you can quickly lose them. If you are not carefully managing them, you may not be able to rely on them whatsoever as they let someone or something else talk them out of maintaining their commitment with you or anyone else.

If you are talking to someone that experiences lesser influences from the outside world, you can safely assume that they are a more controlled, logical, and poised individual. These individuals tend to be excellent leaders, critical thinkers, and intentional in their actions because they know how to win at the game of life. As such, once they make an observation, they generally stick to their original belief because they feel confident in their process. If you can successfully motivate someone like this to get on your team or commit to something with you, you can feel confident that they will remain committed because they take their commitment seriously.

The more someone expresses this level of self-control, the more you need to be intentional about how you interact with them if you ever need to gain something from that person. People with greater self-control are typically knowledgeable in human behavior and engage in analysis themselves on a consistent basis, which means they will be watching you as closely as you are watching them. Being intentional and careful, as well as authentic and full-spirited, ensures your ability to interact with that person in a way they will be positively receptive toward.

It Is Not Your Job To People Please

One thing you have to be cautious with when it comes to analyzing people, especially if you intend to use that analysis to direct your behaviors, is people-pleasing. People pleasers are individuals that read people's baseline and deviations and use that information to manipulate themselves in a way that is intended to make the other person happy. This is rarely done with their own wellbeing in mind; rather, they are focused solely on the wellbeing of the other person. In the end, that person ends up running themselves thin and abandoning themselves and their own needs in favor of everyone else's. You never want to do that to yourself.

It is not your job to people-please. Learning to analyze people is not a step toward people-pleasing; rather, it is a step away from people-pleasing. When you learn to adequately analyze people, you no longer have to assume that it is your responsibility to make them happy because it never was in the first place. Instead, you can understand what they require to reach certain points and offer them guidance to get to that place. This means you end up having your own needs met while effectively collaborating with someone else and their natural personality to get their needs met.

An excellent example of using analysis as a way to avoid people-pleasing, rather than encourage it, would be in a place of business. Let's say you are a manager and you need to pitch your boss on something that would make work much easier for your team; however, your boss does not tend to be the type of person that likes to make changes to the system. If you knew how to analyze him, you could read his behaviors, identify what causes positive deviation, and use that to your advantage so you can encourage him to be in a positive deviation when you ask for the change to be implemented. Chances are, you can get him to "yes" a lot easier this way. The same can be done when it comes to getting any of your wants or needs met, though you should be careful to only ever use this when it creates a positive outcome for everyone if you attempt to manipulate the situation, so your needs are met but no one else's, you will find yourself engaged in negative manipulation, which can be dangerous to yourself and others. This can also create a negative reputation for you, which can be incredibly challenging to get away from once it has been rooted in. You must always think about the good of all, especially if you will be using the analysis to get your way.

CHAPTER 9
Beware Of Cluster Gestures

Cluster gestures is a term used to describe rapid, deviated gestures that a person engages in. These are often quick, short-lived deviations from their baseline that indicate a certain mood or perception toward whichever topic the cluster gestures have happened around. The FBI uses cluster gestures as a way to identify someone's guilt, or other emotional cues, surrounding specific information. This way, they can often tell if someone is lying, covering something up, or feeling guilty about something being discussed with them by the interrogation officers.

Although cluster gestures are commonly looked for by the FBI, they are not exclusively seen in people that are feeling guilty or lying to cover something up. Cluster gestures can also be seen around positive topics and used in positive ways. The primary thing to know about cluster gestures is that the behavior itself is merely a deviation away from baseline for a quick moment. A person will either immediately return to baseline because they want to cover something up or because the overall experience is not about that one topic, so there is no need to retain the emotions or thoughts around it.

Cluster Gestures Occur Around Specific Topics

There are multiple occasions where you might be talking with someone, and the conversation drifts across many different topics. In fact, virtually every conversation you have is likely to drift around multiple topics, even if you are only enjoying short-lived conversations. For example, if you were ordering a coffee at a café, you might start with your order then move on to small talk about the weather or another simple topic. Baseline conversations always deviate, just like people's emotions do.

Cluster gestures can be used as a way to get to know someone better or as a way to get more information out of a person. If you are getting to know someone better, pay close attention to how their gestures are surrounding different topics or pieces of information. This will indicate how they feel about those topics and what their general perspective is toward them. If you are using cluster gestures as a way to get more information out of someone, you will purposefully bring up specific topics to discuss with them so you can monitor their gestures around that topic. This is how authorities use cluster gestures to determine if someone is lying or not, which enables them to prod deeper or dig into other psychological measures to draw information out of potential victims, witnesses, or perpetrators.

If you are using gestures to get to know someone better, you may want to lead the conversation through different topics so you can get to know them from multiple perspectives. You might talk a bit about everything from the wheel of life, which allows you to get a rounded view of who they are, or you may focus exclusively on the parts of the wheel that are relevant to your relationship with that person. The wheel of life defines the eight primary categories of our lives, and it includes health, wealth, career, relationships, love, relationship to yourself, hobbies, and faith.

Suppose you are using cluster gestures as a way to get to know information about a specific topic, such as if you want to know if someone likes something or if they are lying, you want to intentionally bring that topic up and pay close attention to their reaction. If their reaction is neutral, chances are you will not walk away with sufficient information to make your choice. If, however, their reaction is positive or negative, you will walk away with enough knowledge to get a general understanding of their stance on a given subject. This is particularly useful when it comes to surprising someone or catching someone in a lie.

The Type Of Gestures Reveals The Mystery

The way to read the cluster gestures is to pay close attention to the specific types of gestures they are using. You will read their body language, facial expressions, eyes, and emotional energy just as you would in any other circumstance; however, you want to be particularly attentive as cluster gestures are fleeting. If you are prompting them purposefully, you want to do so when you are ready to pay close attention, so you get an adequate analysis for the moment. In many cases, you will see cluster gestures unexpectedly, as this happens on a regular basis and is not always something you have to be looking for or encouraging. Of course, you can use these random moments to deepen your knowledge about someone, which will make your understanding of them more complete. Or, at the very least, it will teach you more about human behavior.

If you are looking to learn about topics that make someone happy or feel positive in some way, pay attention to fleeting cluster gestures that indicate a positive deviation from their baseline. Smiles, eyebrow raises, bright eyes, leaning forward, laughing, or seeming lost in a daydream for a few moments are all great ways to identify a positive reaction. Some people will outright admit to their thoughts or feelings, too, though it is helpful to pay close attention to *how* they admit them to ensure they are telling the truth. This is an excellent way to learn about what lights a person up or makes them feel good, which will allow you to use that information to your advantage. This may help you get your needs met, surprise them, or do something nice for them that helps them feel better if they are having a particularly bad time.

Suppose you are looking for negative deviations, such as if you want to catch someone in a lie, pay close attention to expressions that indicate fear, anxious surprise, anger, sadness, or contempt. A pinched brow, tight face, closed-off posture, or a person leaning away or becoming fidgety all indicates that a person is feeling negative toward a specific sentiment or topic. Sometimes, people may have these reactions because they are feeling guilty or lying about something. Other times, they may be simply expressing distaste or displeasure toward something you have been discussing. Consider the overall conversation and the context behind it to get a clearer understanding of why someone has had a negative deviation, as this will give you greater insight into the thoughts and feelings behind the reaction.

Deviation May Help Uncover The Truth

Deviations are excellent for helping uncover the truth, especially in someone who may be particularly closed off or unwilling to admit to something. When you want to learn the truth from someone, there are three things you can do to leverage cluster gestures as a way to gain insight. You will prod the topic, pay attention to gestures, and recognize their follow up behaviors.

Whenever you prod the topic you want to know more about, it is always best to start small and work your way up. Immediately jumping into the main conversation can be intimidating and may cause someone to be caught off guard, which could make their immediate reaction less accurate. Rather than reacting to the topic itself, they may react to you charging head-first into an intimate or intense conversation.

Instead, you want to work your way there by asking smaller questions that skirt around the conversation itself. Then, you can start working toward the bigger questions. Use the cluster gestures and overall responses you get from the initial questions to guide you through the bigger or more intense questions, never moving faster than the other person is willing to give up information both verbally and nonverbally.

Paying attention to gestures means you have to pay close attention to their body, face, and eyes. Eyes will be the fastest gestures to come and go, followed by the face, then the body. Most people can easily hold a non-assuming posture but struggle to control their face and struggle even more to control their eyes. For that reason, you should look from the eyes to the face, to the body, which ensures that you gain the most information possible. You can immediately begin to uncover what these gestures mean if your knowledge and intuition can guide you, or you can keep track of them in your mind and reflect on them later for deeper understanding. Often, both methods can be used to deepen your insight, if need be.

Lastly, you need to pay attention to their follow up. Someone that is trying to hide something or that has a negative feeling about something will often do their best to change the conversation to something more enjoyable, or they might try to end the conversation altogether.

Alternatively, someone that likes or enjoys something will attempt to have the conversation linger on that topic longer so they can derive more joy from it. A person's follow up will help reinforce their gestures, so pay attention and factor it into your insight when you determine what their actions genuinely mean.

CHAPTER 10
Compare And Contrast What You Discover

The more you observe people and their body language, the more you will discover the meaning of their body language and the best way to interpret it. Recognizing baselines is imperative, yet baselines are irrelevant if you are not using them as they are intended to be used. The purpose of a baseline is to formulate an initial observation about what someone's body language means and how this contributes to their identity profile. Following that initial observation, you need to discover how and why that individual deviates away from their baseline so you can understand their unique body language tendencies.

Believe it or not, body language does have variations from person to person. Similarly to how people speak with varying types of slang, body language can have differences, too. Each person will have their own unique expressions that indicate when they are pleased, annoyed, interested, enraged, and so forth. Recognizing each individual's unique expressions is an excellent way to identify what their body language means and read it more accurately.

The Difference Between Personality And Deviation

Observing the difference between personality and true body language deviations is important because not everyone communicates in the same ways. If you assume everyone communicates the same, you will misinterpret many signals based on irrelevant or inaccurate baseline findings. Instead, you must identify the differences between personality and deviation.

Personality describes the specific ways someone communicates or the body language signals they are most likely to use to communicate with you. For example, a person with a confident personality is likely to use many hand gestures and strong poses, while a person that lacks confidence is likely to stay close to themselves and small in their movements. Knowing this prevents you from misinterpreting a confident person's body language as aggressive or a person without confidence's body language as disinterested because you are aware that the nature of their movements is based on personality, not their mood.

True deviations express an actual shift in emotion or mood that a person experiences. For example, if a person that is typically confident suddenly starts showing signals that they lack confidence, you know they have deviated. These deviations give you significant insight into how a person thinks or feels by showing you that it moves them enough to cause them to actually deviate away from their "normal." These deviations are where you gain the ability to identify the best ways to interact with people. For example, if you want to stimulate a certain emotional response, you can use known triggers to do so. Or, if you want to stimulate more of the same, you can use the necessary triggers.

Each time you meet a new person or start talking to someone, first look for their baseline and personality, then look for deviations. This way, you can clearly interpret each signal and understand what it means, as well as how it will affect your communication with that individual.

Discovering Body Language Nuances

There are two excellent strategies you can use to help you identify body language nuances between different people. Identifying this is essential to discovering people's true baseline, as it allows you to recognize their exact baseline in relation to them. The first strategy allows you to identify nuances and personality differences in an individual, while the second strategy allows you to identify these things over groups of people.

Identifying an individual's nuances is an excellent way to personalize your methods of approaching them and interacting with them based on their personality. When you have a deeper awareness of how someone is and what their methods of expression are, it becomes easier to interpret each of their expressions without questions lingering in your mind as to whether you interpreted correctly or not. You can identify these expressions by observing the person over time, especially in relation to how they react or respond to different triggers in their life. Consider paying close attention to triggers that would typically stimulate an emotional reaction out of someone, and identify how they react to that trigger. Common triggers include stressful situations, hunger, funny jokes, a peaceful view, relaxation, and more. The more you understand a person's natural reactions to different emotions, the easier it will be for you to interpret their thoughts and feelings and the scale to which they are experiencing them.

Identifying an individual's expressions is helpful in that it allows you to understand that person in a more significant manner. However, it is not reasonable to expect yourself to be able to fully understand an individual's nuances and standard body language and behavioral expressions. For example, if you are on a first date with someone, or if you are in a sales meeting, you do not have limitless time to identify how that person communicates and also make an in-depth profile of them. You must learn to read and identify nuances quickly if you want to use body language to your advantage in a more accurate manner. This is where profiling comes in.

Profiling is a practice where you observe as many people as possible, and, as you do, you categorize them. You will rapidly see that people with similar personalities tend to have similar body expressions, too, which means they can be profiled together. Profiling does not guarantee that you have an exact understanding of each individual you meet, but it does provide you with a more complex and accurate baseline of which to interpret people. It also allows you to better understand their deviations, as you are aware of which deviations are likely and normal and how exactly to interpret them based on that person's personality.

Analyzing Each Person's Natural Expressions

Analyzing each person's natural expressions requires patience, as you must be willing to give yourself time to witness these different expressions. One way to do this, especially if you have a significant amount of time with each individual, is to observe their natural reactions to life. This is where you will get the most accurate, in-depth understanding of people's body language because you are observing them in their natural habitat, responding to natural triggers. However, you might not have all the time in the world to observe someone in their natural habitat and wait for each emotion to be naturally invoked.

Once again, dating and sales are two great examples of this. When dating someone, you need to be able to generally identify who they are and how they behave rapidly to determine whether it is worth it for you to go on further dates. In sales, you need to be able to profile someone, so you know how to sell your product or service to them effectively rapidly. Knowing how to prompt people to react to different emotional triggers in a natural way exposes you to their different emotional reactions and gives you the opportunity to understand how their reactions are. The key is you must be in control so you are getting these emotional reactions at the right time, rather than accidentally activating them in a way that has that person thinking they should not be talking to or trusting you any longer.

To prompt someone to express body language relating to a certain emotion, say something that you believe is likely to pull a specific emotional trigger. It is best if you do this based on something they already said to ensure that your desired emotion is triggered. Using something they mentioned upsets them, inspires them, makes them happy, or stimulates any other emotion in them, and says a few things about it. Better yet, ask a question, so they have to engage and think about it. If you do this correctly, they will think in such a way that triggers a specific emotional reaction, and that reaction will help you identify their body language surrounding different emotions.

It is essential to note that the body language they use indicates a lot about how they feel about themselves, too. For example, let's say you elicit feelings of frustration in someone. If you are speaking with a confident person, they will likely expand their body language by puffing out their chest or making themselves appear bigger, which is done as a way to assert their authority and their willingness to protect themselves.

Alternatively, if you are speaking with someone that lacks confidence, they may try to shrink their body language, or they might appear anxious because they do not like to deal with confrontation and anger. Noting the differences is an excellent way to create profiles in your mind so you can adequately interpret different people's body language and signals.

Observing Deviations In Relation To Triggers

To observe someone's deviations in relation to triggers, you must first anticipate what their likely triggers are. Everyone has their own triggers, but most people will have similarities in what triggers them. Family, money, and love or marriage are common triggers in people's lives. Triggers can also be far more specific, such as someone's inability to use a new piece of technology, their favorite food, or an experience they had recently that made them feel either positive or negative.

Anticipating people's likely triggers means you can identify times when they are most likely to deviate from their baseline. You know the minute those triggers are pulled, an emotional response is about to occur, which means you will be able to observe the deviation in their body, face, and movements. You might also pull these triggers on purpose by naturally burying them in your conversation to see what types of emotional responses are gained.

When you observe for deviations, you must pay close attention as deviations can be fleeting, especially if someone is using cluster gestures as a way to cover something up. If you miss someone's cues or signals, you may need to wait for another opportunity to observe them so you understand them better.

If you are purposefully stimulating someone's triggers to create emotional responses, be sure to do so intentionally. For example, in sales, if you are trying to trigger need by stimulating frustration and then offering a solution, pay close attention. You do not want to stimulate too many different emotions, nor do you want to create excess frustration because this makes it seem as though you are intentionally trying to manipulate them. In that case, no one will trust you, and through that, you will lose your capacity to stimulate any emotions other than skepticism and disinterest or frustration toward you.

CHAPTER 11
Observe Mirrored Behaviors

Mirrored behaviors are a unique, interesting form of body language that provides significant insight into how a person thinks or feels about you, specifically. This allows you to move away from reading exclusively about how someone feels about different topics or interests and instead allows you the opportunity to get a better understanding of where you stand with that person. Although this may make it seem deep, mirrored behaviors are not something that requires you to know someone extensively for it to happen. Total strangers may mirror your behavior, as will people you are intentionally engaging with and people you have known for a long time.

When you experience mirrored behaviors, it means the other person is particularly interested in you. The way they mirror your behaviors, the amount they do so, and the specific behaviors they choose to mimic all help you interpret what they actually mean. It helps to understand the context of the situation, the person, and the way they are mirroring you, as this allows you to truly understand where you stand with that person. Mirrored behavior means someone has seen you, taken an interest in you, and is now mirroring your body language. This subconscious behavior makes it obvious that the other person is interested in you and engaged at the moment because they are quite literally mimicking you. Mirrored behavior can happen in physical body language, as well as tonality and speech patterns. The person exhibiting mirrored behavior is engaged with the other person, while the person leading the behavior is generally the one with the upper hand in that conversation. Unless, of course, both parties are mirroring each other's behavior, which shows mutual attraction and interest.

You can observe mirrored behavior in others, as well as yourself. Observing this behavior in yourself may seem strange, as you are becoming self-aware of your own subconscious cues, and it might even feel funny as you realize you are essentially copying the person you are communicating with. Of course, this is a good sign you are on the same page as this person, and it keeps you engaged and subconsciously flatters them, so long as you are not obvious or exaggerated about it. There are four significant times which you might observe mirrored behavior: on a date, during a sale, in general, in everyday life, or in yourself.

Dating And Mirrored Behavior

Looking for mirrored behaviors on a date is an excellent way to gauge how well the date is going and whether it's worth it for you to plan future dates with this person. Romantically speaking, you want a person to be engaged with you and showing interest if you will date them again;

otherwise, you risk investing in someone that is not equally invested in you, which can be a painful experience.

When you go on a date with someone, and they mirror your behavior, it is a sure sign that they are interested in you and are enjoying themselves. Your date is unlikely to be aware of their behavior, so do not go out of your way to point it out to them. Doing so may make them feel uncomfortable and can break the mood and make you both feel awkward. Instead, simply observe it and use it as a sign that they are interested in you or, at the very least, attracted to you.

Observing mirrored behavior in your date's body language will be much easier than observing it elsewhere. They might smile when you smile, touch their hair when you touch yours, or move their arm the same way you do, all without even realizing they are doing it. These are all easy for you to pick up on as you pay attention to their body and what they are doing with it. In verbal language, however, observing mirroring behaviors takes more practice. Mirrored behavior often involves the other person using similar words as you, as well as a similar tone of voice. For example, if you often say "No way!" excitedly, and you say something to your date, and they say "No way!" with excitement in their tone, you can feel confident that a person is attracted to you and interested in knowing more about you.

Mirrored Behavior And Sales

Salespeople often use mirrored behavior as a way to gauge the level of interest of their audience, as well as to identify the exact moment that one should pitch their sale. When a client is mirroring your body language, it means they are interested in what you have to say and are eager to learn more. The sooner a person starts mirroring your body language, and the more engaged they are, the easier they will be to sell to. This doesn't mean you should get complacent or assume they are an automatic yes; however, it does signify that this client has significant potential to become a purchasing client.

Using mirrored behavior in sales means identifying how you can use it to pinpoint the exact moment you should make your pitch. This means you must observe not only mirrored behavior but also the amount of mirrored behavior being expressed. You must observe carefully to pinpoint the moment mirrored behavior starts and to track it so you can identify when it becomes more frequent. Once a person is frequently mirroring your behavior and matching your expressions, you know they are ready for you to pitch to.

With sales, mirrored behavior is less likely to be sensual in nature. Unlike with dates, where your date may focus on their hair or grooming themselves, your client is more likely to mimic your excited and happy behaviors. They might smile, mimic your hand gestures, or match your words as a way to show they are engaged in your pitch. All of this will be happening subconsciously, so they are unlikely to realize they have changed their expressions at all. Of course, don't point this out. Instead, quietly observe and use it to help you pace the conversation and pitch your offer.

Mirrored Behavior In General

Outside of dating and sales, mirrored behavior can still happen. Often, it signifies attraction or interest in someone, so you are most likely to notice it when you engage with someone who is invested in you at that moment. The most common place to see mirrored behavior in your everyday life is amongst your friends and family, though you may also see it between coworkers, especially if you are in competition with any of them. With friends or family, mirrored behaviors are an expression of the mutual love shared between you and the people you care about and can be seen as endearing and an affirmation of your connection.

With coworkers that you are in competition with, not ones you are friends with, mirrored behaviors indicate they want to be like you, but better. Essentially, they are mirroring the behaviors they see you engaging in that boost your likelihood of succeeding, then adding their own added abilities to make themselves look better. In this case, mirrored behavior is conscious, not subconscious, because that person is intentionally trying to mimic your behaviors.

One other time you might see mimicry or mirrored behaviors is with someone that looks up to you. When people look up to you or idolize you, they start mimicking your behaviors because they desire to be just like you. This is a wonderful example of "mimicry is the highest form of flattery" because it implies that they are inspired by you and want to be more like you.

Mirroring Other's Behavior

Mirroring another person's behavior on purpose is an excellent way to gain someone's attention or get them more invested in you. Just as someone's subconscious mind is responsible for them mirroring you, their subconscious mind also interprets your mirrored behaviors of them and uses it to reinforce that they are liked at that moment. They can see you are invested in them, and they become more invested in you as a result. This is an excellent way to gain someone's investment by mildly mirroring their behavior until they start to do it back, which means they are paying attention and interested.

If you choose to use mirrored behaviors to support your ability to attract engagement from others, you must be careful. Excessive mirroring or using strange behaviors in an effort to motivate mirroring are both unnatural ways that people attempt to identify this type of behavior, and that can sabotage your communications. You must learn to infuse this practice into natural communication to avoid confusing people or driving them away.

It is important to mirror behaviors relevant to the context of your meeting, too, to avoid using behaviors that are unnatural to the circumstances. For example, if you are on a date, mirror your date when they smile, groom their hair, or fix their clothes. Or, if you are in a sales meeting, mirror your client any time they use certain hand gestures, words, or facial expressions. This way, you match in a way that is appropriate to the circumstances, which makes them feel even more invested in a positive way. Once someone is mirroring you consistently, you do not have to worry about mirroring them back, as you have now gained their investment.

CHAPTER 12
Identify The Strong Voice

Each person has their own unique voice, or the voice they use on a regular basis. Discovering their strong voice, or primary voice, allows you to learn more about this person based on what you hear in the sound of their voice. Each person expresses a great deal about themselves, from their personality to their self-perception and emotions, which is why their voices are so valuable. Knowing what someone's voice means, means you can use it to help you interpret that person and gain insight into them through your conversation.

Like with body language, voices have a baseline (strong voice) and deviations. Knowing the baseline of someone's voice means you can identify their deviations. How you interpret these deviations are just like interpreting deviations in physical gestures: as long as you know what is normal, you can identify what isn't and listen for cues to understand *why* it was no longer normal. Most often, emotions or beliefs are the driving force behind deviations and provide ample reason for someone to suddenly start speaking or sounding different.

The Meaning Of Tonality And Why It Matters

Tonality refers to a person's voice, and the tone of their voice reflects their different emotions and characteristics. You can identify a person's tonality through written language, as well as the spoken language. A person's baseline tonality gives you the opportunity to better understand their average personality, while their deviations allow you to interpret their emotions and perceptions around different topics, just like with body language.

It is important to understand that tonality changes a lot under different circumstances. For example, the way your voice sounds when you talk to your family will be far different from how it sounds when you talk to your boss. These different tones are used to assert different emotions while also positioning yourself in different roles. With your family, you might be positioning yourself casually, while with your boss, you might be positioning yourself as a confident worker.

Just as your tonality will change, so will others tones. Listening for variances allows you to identify how a person likely sees themselves in relation to another person, how they want to come across to that person, and what emotion they are feeling at that moment. This is important, as the more you understand a person, the easier it is to relate to them and use this relation to gain what you want from them.

Interpreting someone's tonality is essential to the process of analyzing people because of the amount of knowledge you gain from this form of analysis. While body language and facial expressions may prove tough to interpret from time to time, tonality is almost always easy to identify and read. Your brain subconsciously knows how to interpret most tones, and you can use certain expressions and indicators to ensure that you have interpreted it correctly.

Another reason why interpreting tonality is so important is that, in our modern world, distant communications are common. We tend to spend more time talking on the phone, texting, or connecting over social media or email than we do talking to people in person. Knowing how to interpret tonality through text and written language means you can better understand that person from a distance and use that to your advantage for whatever you might need it for.

Identifying A Person's Typical Tone

Identifying a person's typical tone is as important as identifying their baseline body language, as it provides you the opportunity to understand what their "normal" is. Knowing their normal immediately indicates what personality archetype they have and what you can likely expect out of that person. This way, you can anticipate reactions to different emotional triggers and use their baseline to determine whether their reaction was normal to their behavior or not. You can also use this to identify the occurrence of a reaction in the first place, which can be especially helpful when you want or need to stimulate specific reactions out of people. Even when you don't, witnessing this allows you to understand that person with greater context and dynamics.

The easiest way to identify a person's typical tone is to strike up a conversation with them and listen. Talk about everything from small talk topics to topics that are more relevant to the context of your meeting, and listen to see how they come across. What personality traits can you identify through their tone? How do you think they position themselves in the conversation, based on how they sound? Is there anything to indicate that they are feeling affected by something beyond the conversation and that they may be bringing that forth with them? You can interpret all of these answers based on the projection of their voice, the emotions you pick up on, and how readily willing they are to speak to you.

If you are speaking online or through text, pay attention to how their punctuation looks, which words they are using, and what they have said overall. Emojis are another great way to interpret tone, as people who use a lot of emojis tend to have more whimsical or light-hearted personalities and will directly convey their intended emotion or tone through the emojis they add to their conversation. However, emojis are not always appropriate to the communication forum, so be aware of people using them inappropriately as this may indicate they are not taking something seriously or are uneducated in that style of communication.

The Common Triggers Of Tonality

Once you know someone's baseline, you can identify anytime their tonality changes from what you have come to see as being normal. Change in tonality gives you two things: the opportunity to know more about a person and the opportunity to gauge them. When it comes to getting to know a person, change in tonality gives you more context behind their methods of interacting and allows you to identify how they feel and view themselves in different circumstances. This is a great way to have more compassion, a deeper understanding, or a more significant ability to anticipate a person. When it comes to gauging them, tonality allows you to identify how a person feels at that moment to see whether it is worth it for you to make a pitch. So, if you are selling something or want to receive something from someone, you can use their tone to determine whether they're ready or not.

There are many things that will trigger tonality change. The four most likely triggers are other people, circumstances, their location, or the context in which they have shown up for something.

Other people trigger a change in tonality because the person who is talking views themselves differently around others, so their role changes. For example, at one moment, they may be playing the role of parent, while in another, they may be the friend or the confidante. As their role changes, their tone changes, too, to match the role they have taken on.

Circumstances trigger a change in tonality by first triggering the emotions a person experiences. Specific circumstances might also cause a person to pick a new role in relation to the circumstance, which further stimulates change. For example, in a casual setting, someone might sound casual, but as soon as they are presented with a task to complete, they take on a more authoritative role.

Location triggers change in tonality based on habit. People usually associate different locations with different roles in their lives, which they tend to click into regardless of whether they are actively in need of playing out that role or not. For example, at home, you might continue to be authoritative and parental, even if your children are not around because you habitually associate home with parenting.

Context triggers change in tonality by giving the person a story, or a reason, behind why they have shown up for something. When a person has a story in mind about why they have shown up, they formulate a role to suit that story, and they partake in that role. For example, if you call a friend over for a casual dinner, they will likely show up in a casual manner, but if you call them over to vent about something difficult you have faced, they might show up with a more concerned or focused tone.

Discovering The Meaning Of Their Tone

Observing the meaning of someone's tonality gives you the opportunity to use that tone to formulate an assumption about that person. This does not guarantee your assumption is right, but it allows you to use that assumption as a baseline so you can then look for clues to determine if you were right or not. You discover the meaning of someone's tone by observing their tone and listening for specific cues about what their tone actually is in any given moment.

There are five essential types of tones when it comes to communication, all of which give you ample insight into how a person is feeling or perceiving themselves in any circumstance. The five tones include motivator, educator, coach, colleague, and caretaker. People may often match two or more of these descriptions at any moment; however, they will always have one primary tone in each setting. Which primary tone will change based on their triggers, too, so observe for these changes to gain more information about someone.

The tone of the motivator often sounds like an inspirational person. They tend to say things that are uplifting and inspiring, and their voice comes across as cheery and hopeful. You can hear the cheer in their voice based on the sheer energy behind it, and they tend to project their voice with certainty and excitement. A motivator sounds enthused about everything. Depending on who they are talking to, they may be motivational in that they are coaching someone else to achieve greatness, or motivational in that they are motivated to receive coaching from someone else to achieve greatness. A great example of a motivator would be Michelle Obama or Oprah Winfrey, both of which are excellent at inspiring others through their tonality and expressions.

Educator tonality indicates that someone knows something and wants to inform others. Their voice is full of authority, and they speak in affirmatives. They make statements more than anything else, and when they ask a question, it is intentional and to reinforce their point. An educator will rarely speak with elation or excitement because these two might indicate they are not in control or in a position of authority. Instead, they have a rather consistent tone, and the ends of their sentences tend to have a consistent pitch, rather than an upturn in the pitch of their voice. A great example of an educator would be Martin Luther King Jr., who was a motivational educator. His primary communication style was as an educator, as he informed people of what was going on and used this information to inspire change.

A coaching tone sounds directive and assertive and will vary depending on whether it is uplifting or demanding based on the coach's personality. Because it is directive and assertive, it often sounds like a coach is bossing you around or making commands, rather than pausing to receive feedback. A positive coach recognizes that their role is to lead everyone else, so they will confidently tell everyone what to do. If they are an excellent coach, they will ask for feedback and receive input from their team to ensure they are directing them in a way that motivates their team to listen and take action. The inclusion of this spoken behavior indicates they are a caring coach that sees themselves as a part of the team rather than an authoritative coach that sees themselves as being above the team. An excellent example of a coach is Tony Robbins, who knows how to communicate to get everyone involved while also operating as a part of his team, rather than being above his team.

The tonality of a colleague is one that is chatty and informal, and that sees you as being equal to them. They often speak similarly to you and will have a neutral or uplifted tone in their voice as they come across as friendly and warm. You know a colleague feels equal to you because they will inspire you while also being inspired by you. Virtually everything about your communication is equal, which means they view you as being on the same level as they are. Because of this, your communication is balanced and often rather enjoyable while also being potentially insightful and helpful. An excellent example of a colleague is your best friend or your closest workmate, both of which will likely speak to you in a casual, informal manner.

If someone has a caretaker tone, their tone comes across as concerned and careful. Their voice almost sounds whiny as they ask if you are ok and try to help you through whatever trouble you may be facing. They sound concerned, often speak in a higher pitch, and will say things that indicate they are willing to take care of you mentally, emotionally, or physically. A caretaker sees themselves as being responsible for others and feels the need to look after everyone around them. If a caretaker takes this tone on in appropriate circumstances, such as when they are parenting, they see themselves as being responsible for another and are genuinely caring. If they take this role on when it is seemingly inappropriate, such as with their boss or a colleague, it indicates that they see themselves as less than and believe they are responsible for everyone. This is a good sign that they feel unworthy or uncomfortable around others. A great example of a caretaker would be one of your parents, which allows you to observe the nuances in their caretaking behaviors and tones throughout the process of caring for you in different circumstances.

CHAPTER 13
Pay Attention To Their Walk

You can tell a significant amount about a person based on the way they walk. Everything from the way they stand to the way they move their body while walking reveal key factors about their personality and who they likely are. Each of us has our own walk and will put our own flair and style into it. The way that flair or style comes across is how you determine what a person's walk genuinely says about them.

As with anything else, the way a person walks can change based on the context of the situation and the way they are feeling. For example, a generally peppy person that is feeling sad or disempowered may suddenly start to walk more slouched over and slow, or a generally shy person that is feeling confident or empowered may start to walk taller and with greater authority. Paying attention to someone's normal and deviations from normal, then, is still a key role in reading someone's walk properly.

Aside from paying attention to baselines and deviations, there are seven key pieces of information you can gain from a person's walk. These pieces of information give you an insight into their personality, behaviors, and tendencies and can help you make more sense of a person in your life. You can also use these factors to help you create a walk that communicates precisely what you want people to think about you, allowing you to have a subconscious impact on the way people perceive you.

Their Speed Correlates To Their Energy

The speed at which someone walks says a great deal about the amount of energy they bring to their lives or at least the amount of energy they are bringing at that moment. If a person typically walks faster, this indicates that they generally have high energy and are highly outgoing. Fast walkers have actually been studied and reported as being more conscientious, having a lower rate of neuroticism, and higher rates of extraversion. They also tend to be more open to the world around them and are excellent socializers. If you are looking for an outgoing, life-of-the-party type person, look for someone that moves fast. If someone suddenly starts moving faster, though they generally walk slower, this may indicate one of two things. They may suddenly have improved energy and are feeling good about something, or they may be anxious or worried about something.

It is important to note the type of fastness that we're looking for here. Fast yet graceful indicates that said individual typically walks faster; therefore, they are naturally more outgoing. If a person is walking fast and lacks grace, however, either because they are stumbling or they just plain look strange doing it, this indicates they do not generally walk fast. Chances are, this is someone that is trying to get somewhere in a hurry.

Slow Speed Indicates A Cautious Personality

A person that walks at a particularly slow pace or that tends to stroll when they walk, no matter where they are walking, is someone that tends to have a more cautious personality. This person feels uncertain and uncomfortable about things; therefore, they are walking slower, so they have more time to process and create feelings of safety. People that walk slowly as a sign of cautiousness are generally not expressing that they are suddenly troubled; rather, they are genuinely slower, more cautious people that require more time to figure things out. If a person suddenly starts walking slower than normal, this might indicate they are upset or feeling down about something.

In addition to a slower overall pace, a person that is generally more cautious will take shorter steps. It is as though they are truly trying to move forward slowly, the way one might carefully step toward the edge of a high cliff or across a balance beam when they are feeling unsteady. They want time to pace themselves and come to terms with each step, rather than to rush through it. This type of person is generally measured, fiercely independent, and self-centered, though this may not mean they experience these tendencies in a negative way. For example, they may be self-centered but not self-serving, meaning they do tend to focus on themselves, but they are still kind and caring toward others.

If They're Anxious, They Veer To The Left

A person that is feeling anxious may be obvious in their hunched shoulders, reduced space expenditure, and fidgety behavior. Even if they manage to calm themselves enough that they're not taking fast, short strides, a person that is feeling anxious can still be identified by their walk. Their key identifying factor is that, if they are anxious, they will veer to the left. This is true whether they are generally anxious overall or just anxious in that particular moment.

This peculiar insight was gained when researchers placed a blindfold over people's eyes and had them walk around in an empty room. Those that were feeling anxious tended to veer to the left while no one else did. Researchers proposed this may be the case because, during a moment of anxiety, the right side of your brain works harder than the left side of your brain as it has to manage the instance of doubt and dread. Regardless of whether that's true or not, you can observe this in people in real life, too.

Confidence Can Be Seen In A Saunter

Sauntering can be seen by anyone that walks slow and easy, with a sense of swagger in their step. They walk as though they are the coolest person in the world because, in their worlds, they are the coolest. These individuals have a high sense of self-confidence and believe greatly in themselves and their abilities. You might assume this to be reserved for high-end professionals and athletes, yet this can actually be seen in any type of human.

The walk of confidence cannot be missed because of how tall and significant it is. In fact, we are so accustomed to seeing and interpreting this walk as confidence that many therapists have begun using this as a way to improve their client's confidence. They start by having the client visualize themselves walking with confidence, then move toward having them walk this way in real life. As the client grows used to seeing themselves this way with visualization, they feel a greater sense of self-confidence. As they grow used to walking this way, they experience biofeedback that tells their brain that they are confident; therefore, they feel a more significant sense of confidence.

Agitated Walkers Are Detail-Oriented

People that walk with a sense of agitation, or like they are harried, have quick bursts of energy in their walk. They tend to move fast, to the point where they almost look fidgety or reactive. Often, they are doing more than just walking, too. They may be fixing their clothes, checking their bag, texting, talking on the phone, reaching for a taxi, or doing all of these things at once. People that walk this way are reported as having greater attention to detail than the average person, which is why their brains are always running so fast.

In addition to walking with a seeming sense of agitation or excess energy, these walkers tend to jump into action faster than anyone else, too. They are the first to jump up and open the door, pull out a chair for someone, or shake someone's hand. Their quick, jerky walking style pivots their attention from one place to another as they go, and that helps their thoughts race through their mind, too. These people are highly effective and productive, which makes them excellent professionals or people to have in charge of special projects.

Self-Esteem Can Be Witnessed In Grace

The amount of self-esteem a person experiences can be directly witnessed in a person's grace. Still, this is not always the most accurate way to tell someone's self-confidence levels, as many people are excellent at mimicking grace as a way to appear more confident than they actually are. It is said, however, that a person that walks more gracefully tends to have a greater sense of self-esteem and self-confidence.

Beyond gracefully gliding through each step, you will actually witness this type of person display grace in their posture, too. Their toes will be intentionally pointed, they seem to swiftly carry their whole body through with each step, and they look as though they are dancing as they walk. This type of walking is said to be unnatural to our bodies, which means a person must learn to intentionally walk this way, thus affirming their high self-esteem and self-confidence.

The Position Of Their Shoulders Says This...

Lastly, the position of someone's shoulders says a lot about how they are feeling. A person that walks with tall, squared shoulders likely feels confident in themselves, at least to the point of intentionally correcting their posture as they walk. A person that walks with tall, casual shoulders naturally feels good about themselves, as this is how they genuinely walk and are not postured intentionally. A person that walks with their shoulders down or slumped is trying to protect themselves. The position of their shoulders indicates they are trying to physically protect their hearts because they are vulnerable or they carry hurt around them.

Sometimes, people that have recently experienced trauma or something that reduces their self-esteem or mood will begin walking with slumped shoulders. Often, this is a temporary change and will revert back once they heal, though this may become their new normal if the experience was traumatizing enough.

CHAPTER 14
Be Aware Of Action Words

The words people choose when communicating with others' say a lot about their personality. Unlike other forms of body language or communication, the specific words people use to communicate and describe things typically remain the same. For this reason, it is helpful to be mindful of action words, as well as any words a person frequently uses, as this all indicates how they think and who they are.

Action words become particularly helpful when you have someone describe something. For example, if you are out with a friend and ask them to describe how their day went, the specific words they use will say a lot about what they genuinely think about their answer. Using their word choice to analyze them and what they mean is an excellent way to gain context into how they actually think or feel about something. Thus, you gain the opportunity to either know them more or use their own language to communicate with them more effectively.

What "I" Really Means About You

The word "I" says more about people than they tend to realize. In fact, the impact it has on our perception of ourselves and other people's perception of us is massive. Yet, many people do not realize this because of the impact it is having, and the experience of saying "I" itself are two highly subconscious experiences. You do not realize how often you say it, and others tend not to realize how frequently they hear it; instead, they just pick up on a "vibe" from you.

The vibe they're picking up on is often quite selfish. Saying "I" frequently indicates that you are focused more on yourself than anything, which means you may be expressing the fact that you are subordinate to everyone around you. By saying "I" frequently, others can tell that you are fixated on yourself, which generally means you are feeling anxious, self-conscious, or insecure. In fixating on yourself, you hope to shield yourself by owning your flaws and explaining them away to the best of your ability, which allows you to feel as though you are protected. Despite this fact, you might otherwise come across as confident. This is because people that are insecure are often trying the hardest to appear as though they are not, which is why they come across as arrogant and egotistical since their confidence is not rooted and genuine.

People that avoid the word "I" are found as being higher powered and as having significant confidence. They have so much confidence in themselves that they do not need to think about themselves or worry excessively about their self-awareness. Rather than busying themselves with the worry of how they are and what they look like, they are excited about the world outside of themselves and are looking for ways to engage in it. They tend to say "you" and "we" more or will use sentences that do not refer to anyone in particular, whatsoever.

Slang And Casual Language

Slang and casual language play a significant role in the way people view us. Our slang and casual language are influenced by our location, culture, or religion, the people we hang out with most, and our interests. On a grander scale, slang says more about our origin story than anything else. When we get down to specific types of slang, though, or "niche" slang, then we start revealing aspects of our personality traits or interests.

The degree to which our slang creates our origin story depends on how similarly we talk to the people in our locale. For example, people from New York talk far differently from people in Los Angeles. Likewise, people in the United States talk differently from people in Canada or Europe. These wider-scale nuances indicate where we are from, and to a trained ear, may even indicate where we are from in our locale. An excellent example would be the many vernaculars from New York, as people from different neighborhoods speak quite differently. If you were not from New York, you might recognize differences but not know what they mean. If you were a regular in New York, though, you would be able to tell which neighborhood they were from solely based on the way a person spoke.

Niche slang can further your ability to profile people by giving you the opportunity to identify their interests and the type of people they hang out with. For example, someone that hangs out with people in the music industry and that loves producing audio would use slang words that were associated with music, audio, and pop culture. Their use of these words would far exceed anyone that was not genuinely interested in this industry.

Listening to the slang words a person uses, as well as their casual language, allows you to understand more about who they are and where they come from. Once you put together their origin with their likely interests, you get a clearer understanding of what their personality is like, what they are interested in, and what they value or cherish. All of this can be used to gain context around a person's personality and show you the ways to connect with that person effectively.

Action Words That Declare Values

Action words declare things in someone's life or give you some insight into what they value. In conversations, action words describe things. People tend to use specific describing words or action words that hint toward their personality while also giving you the opportunity to understand more of what they value in life.

To identify someone's personality through action words, pay close attention to the types of words they use to describe the things that happen in their life. They may describe very few things, suggesting they are closed, cautious, and disinterested in what they are talking about. Or, they may describe many things while using colorful language to describe said things, which indicates they are fascinated, open, and engaged with the world around them. This may also indicate that they are a people pleaser or that they use highly open language to prevent people from asking more personal questions. This way, people think they know enough and do not need to ask anything more personal.

The average person will describe things, but not with extensive detail, and only when a description seems to naturally fit the conversation. The types of describing words they use indicate their generation, as well as the level of energy they bring with them in life. You may also discover what their personality is like, whether it is fun, flamboyant, proper, artistic, or otherwise, based on the types of action words they use.

To discover more of what they value in life, pay attention to where and when they use action words. The average person will only describe the things they care about and will provide more detail based on the amount they care about said thing. Listen to the types of words they use to describe said things to understand their energy around it, too. For example, if they use strong words filled with strong emotion, they are describing something they are seriously passionate about. If they describe things mildly and with casual emotion, this indicates they are interested in something, but not as extensively as they could be.

Matching People's Words

Matching people's words is a surprisingly common behavior, which falls under the category of mirrored behaviors. Couples can often tell which friend their spouse has been hanging out with recently, based on the language their partner is using when they return. When we like someone and have a good time with them, we tend to pick up the words they use and often incorporate them into our own language, too. We subconsciously talk the same way others' do as a way to create familiarity and a connection, and we often carry that into our own lives even once we are no longer around that other person. Often, we go back to our normal way of speaking after a few hours or days, though we may incorporate someone else's language into our own if we are particularly affectionate toward that person.

If you want to connect with someone intentionally, matching their words is an excellent way to do so. By describing things to them in a way they understand, and in the same way they would have described it, you connect with them. Through this, you know they understand you because you have said it in "their language." This way, they connect with you more, pay closer attention to what you are talking about, and have positive responses.

CHAPTER 15
Be Aware Of Personality Clues

Depending on what theory you look into, there are thousands of personality archetypes. However, the most popular theory in the world of psychology is the Jungian theory, which defines 12 Jungian archetypes. These 12 archetypes describe different personalities people are most likely to have, which allows you to have a better awareness of the type of people you are dealing with. Each personality type can be identified by key clues that indicate how that person is and who they are at their core. Of course, each archetype will have several subtypes that define the people within it; however, you will see massive similarities between these groups of people.

It is crucial to note that each person will likely fit into multiple personality type categories; however, they will have one that stands out above the rest. This personality type is the one you need to be aware of, as it indicates their overarching approach to life. If they have a strong secondary and tertiary personality type, use these to gain greater context around who they are and how they are.

The Ruler

The ruler is said to be a more independent type of person, and they thrive on having the most power possible. They want to be the leader, in control of everything around them. Their driving force is wanting control, and their goals involve prosperity and success in virtually every area of their lives. The ruler archetype uses their power as a strategy, and their greatest fear is chaos or being overthrown by the people they are leading. At their worst, the ruler can become highly authoritative to the point of it being destructive, and they struggle to delegate tasks. They are excellent with leadership and responsibility and work excellently in places of leadership. CEOs, bosses, aristocrats, politicians, role models, administrators, managers, and the monarchy are all known for having the ruler archetype.

The Artist

The artist is deeply in tune with their soul energy. They are excellent at imagining things and then promptly creating them. Often, they are seen as being the best at realizing visions or manifesting people's dreams into reality. Their fear would be mediocrity or execution, especially if it was caused by their creations. They use their artistic skill and control to manipulate the world around them, and they long to create cultures and express their vision to the world. The artist archetype tends to fall victim to their own perfectionism and may use bad solutions as a way to fix problems in their lives solely because those solutions provided space for creativity. When they are in their prime, artists are excellent with creativity and imagination and often find themselves in careers involving art, creation, invention, or planning.

The Sage

The sage is another self-driven person that tends to find themselves in isolation or independence more often than not. They are inspired by the truth and seek the truth in everything they do. Their intelligence and ability to analyze allow them to understand the world around them, and they use this as a strategy by seeking out information, engaging in self-reflection, and lusting after personal development and growth. They are terribly afraid of being duped, misled, or of falling victim to ignorance, especially if they themselves are the ignorant ones. Their weakness is that they can become trapped in analysis paralysis, but if they let that go, they are exceptional with offering wisdom and sharing their intelligence. The sage archetype commonly works in roles like scholars, teachers, detectives, advisors, planners, researchers, and anything to do with academics.

The Innocent

The innocent archetype is driven heavily by their ego. They want to be free to be themselves and desire freedom for everyone else, too. This archetype wants to get to paradise; they love living innocent and simplistic lifestyles, experiencing all of the good things the world has to offer. The number one goal of the innocent is to be happy, and they are afraid of being pushed to do something bad or wrong by the people in their lives. The strategy, often followed by an innocent person, is to do things right the first time because they do not want things to be done wrong. Because of how innocent they tend to be, this archetype is often seen as boring by others and rarely engages in things that others would deem fun or enjoyable. They are not the "life of the party" type. This archetype is particularly talented with faith and optimism and tends to be employed in traditional jobs such as teachers, lawyers, doctors, and so forth.

The Explorer

The explorer is a soul-driven person that loves to enjoy the freedom and the ability to adventure around the world. This type of person wants to learn about who they are through the world around them and uses adventure as a way to deepen their understanding of themselves. They tend to be highly outgoing and enjoy meeting new people and gaining new perspectives on life, as this serves their minds with a sense of adventure, too. The biggest fear of an explorer is to be trapped, experience conformity to the world around them, or endure a sense of inner emptiness. They want to live a fulfilling, authentic, unique life that teaches them plenty. The weakness of the explorer is to find themselves lost or aimless or becoming a misfit to the world around them. They may also start to run away from their fears in an effort to protect themselves. You can often find the explorer archetype working as a freelancer, blogging, and jumping between small projects as they find work wherever they go.

The Rebel

The rebel is another soul-driven type, meaning they live from their soul and a place of deep authenticity. This person believes rules were made to be broken and will frequently try to convince other people to break the rules with them. They believe in getting revenge or revolting against things and will overturn anything that isn't working, even if they are the only ones it isn't working for. They fear being powerless or ineffective at gaining their desires and use the strategies of disruption, destruction, and shock to get their way. If they are not careful, the rebel archetype can start getting into trouble with the law and engaging in crimes because they long so hard to be on the "wrong side" of things. This person will often work in careers that give them an adrenaline rush, or they will make their money under the table, so they don't have to pay "the man" for their earnings.

The Hero

The hero type is another egotistical archetype. This person always comes to the rescue of others because they get a boost to their ego when they realize they are powerful enough to be needed by others. They believe they can get through anything and will always find a way to accomplish anything that someone needs. They want to prove their worth to others through their acts of heroism and seek to master things that will improve the world for others. They are terrified of being weak, vulnerable, or scared, especially in situations where others' could witness these feelings in them. The hero archetype uses their strength and competency as a strategy and is talented with being courageous and confident. They often work as firefighters, cops, politicians, activists, non-profit organization leaders, eco-friendly CEOs, and other activist-oriented roles.

The Magician

The magician is a self-type, meaning they have a strong relationship with themselves, and they are their own driving factor. This archetype believes in their ability to make anything happen and is excellent at getting everything they want in life. Their number one goal is to understand the fundamental laws of the universe and use these laws to their ability. They also want to make dreams come true, regardless of whose dreams they might be. They are afraid of enduring unintended negative consequences from their actions, especially because they can become so fixated on getting what they want to the point they will do it at any cost. If they are not careful, the magician can be highly manipulative, and people may dread being around that person. When they learn to develop a vision and live by it, this archetype is excellent with finding win-win solutions and using their magic for everyone's benefit. They are frequently employed as inventors, planners, and researchers. Magicians also find themselves in medicine, including alternative medicine, and as charismatic leaders in new-age businesses.

The Jester

The jester is the last of the four types that are driven by their own presence. They are the humorous type and believe that you only live once, so you might as well have fun with the time you have. They love to experience the joy of every moment and live for the fulfillment of life. Their goal is to have fun and make the world a lighter, funnier place for everyone around them. They are afraid of being bored or of being boring to others, so they are always spontaneously jumping around, keeping themselves occupied, and serving humor to everyone they meet. With playing, joking, and being funny, the jester archetype can find their way through anything. They can, however, succumb to being frivolous and wasting time, which can prevent them from reaching their goals. They are often employed in positions where they can play and have fun, or they have lower positions in their careers but enjoy their work because they are constantly bringing fun into it for themselves and everyone around them. The jester archetype will often become known as the office prankster and will be admired and appreciated by most.

The Everyman

The everyman is an egotistical archetype. Their primary belief is everyone was created equally, and they desire to connect with other people. The number one goal of an everyman is to belong somewhere, and they will do anything they can to feel as though they fit in with the world around them. They are afraid of being left out or standing alone from the rest of the crowd, and they project this fear onto others, which is what drives their inclusivity. Their strategy is developing ordinary virtues and remaining down to earth, which makes them seem as though they fit in with everyone else. The everyman is at high risk of losing themselves in an effort to blend in, and they can find themselves in superficial relationships if they are not careful. They are excellent with realism, empathy, and a lack of pretense and regularly find themselves in careers that serve their community or where they get to work hard for a living.

The Lover

The lover is a soul-driven archetype that believes heavily in romance and living life with another individual. They tend to find their partner and live with that person as a significant part of their life, to the point where they may make other couples feel jealous of their great connection. The lover desires to be intimate and to experience the love and presence of another. They always want to be in a relationship and long to be surrounded by people, places, and things they love. If they cannot feel the passion for something they're doing, they don't want to be doing it. Their greatest fear is being alone or unwanted, or of finding out someone doesn't love them. They always do their best to become more physically and emotionally attractive, so people are interested in them and pay closer attention. They are passionate, grateful, appreciative, and committed. They often work jobs that fulfill their individual passions, and that allows them to bring their entire sensuality into the experience. Fashion designers, spa workers, and team-builders all tend to be the lover archetype.

The Caregiver

Caregivers are the fourth and final variety of the ego-driven archetype. They believe in loving others the same way they would love themselves and want everyone to feel their best. The caregiver feels their best when they are protecting and caring for others, and will often push themselves into caregiving positions so they can look after other people. Their number one goal is to help others, and they do so by physically taking over and doing things for other people. They fear being selfish or not being able to express adequate gratitude in their lives, and at their weakest, they can become martyrs or be exploited for their generosity. At their strongest, they are highly compassionate and generous, which helps them in their typical career paths as nurses, care aides, support workers, and assistants.

CHAPTER 16
Never Forget To Put It Together!

Independently, each piece of information you gain from analyzing a person will not say much. If you fixate on one signal, you will gain a limited understanding of why that signal is being made or what it means. You must take the time to look across a person's entire presentation to understand more about them and gain a more accurate insight into who they are and why they are expressing themselves the way they are.

At first, it may take practice to adequately put together all the cues, to the point where you reflect on experiences long after they ended. This reflection is excellent, as it allows you to give context to the many things I have taught you within this book. Eventually, you will rapidly view all the signals and put them together, in context, to create your analysis findings. You will reach this point rapidly, so don't worry about taking your time and thoroughly researching each step. Once you start observing people in action, it comes fast.

First Step: Physical Cues

The first thing you want to do is look for physical cues on a person. Before you even say hello, you have the opportunity to look at their body and gain an understanding of how they are feeling at that moment. Pay attention to their posture, where they have positioned themselves, what shared environment you are in, and what they are doing within that environment. If they happen to be moving or making gestures, pay attention to those, as well.

Whether you realize it or not, you already have an opinion of someone formulated in your subconscious mind, well before you actually talk to that person. Giving yourself an intentional moment to look at their behavior, understand their expressions, and make an opinion is an excellent way to lay the foundation of your analysis.

Once you start interacting with a person, pay attention to how their behavior is. They may remain the same, or their behavior may shift as they are now connecting with a new individual. This is a great way to rapidly gain insight into that person's baseline and who they are, so you can start to identify nuances in their behavior and deviations from their regular.

Second Step: Emotional Cues

Emotional cues can be spotted in body language, facial expressions, tone of voice, words chosen, and the overall energy of a person you are communicating with. Ideally, you want to spot the emotional cues of a person before you start talking to them or early into the conversation, so you know what to expect. Knowing someone's emotional cues means you can adjust your behavior accordingly, to be compassionate toward their emotions. If you are trying to gain something out of them, this also gives you the opportunity to create the right emotional response to have them synchronized with you and following what you are saying.

People's emotional cues can rapidly change; for example, upon seeing you, they may click into a different emotional state than they were in prior to you arriving or introducing yourself. Paying attention to these shifts helps you understand someone, the way they are feeling, and the things they are enjoying about your conversation. You can also spot what they are averse to or what they are avoiding, based on their negative emotional response factors.

Third Step: Vocal Cues

Once someone starts talking, you want to pay attention to their vocal cues. People will tell you how they are feeling in their tone of voice, expressions, word choice, pace, and the amount to which they share. Listening to someone's voice for clues to how they are feeling and what they need lets you validate any assumptions you have made until this point. They also help add more context to a person and deepen your understanding of how they feel or what they think.

Vocal cues will be most likely to deviate from baseline energy and are easiest for people to lie about, so be careful when listening to a person's voice. You might hear an energy "behind" their voice, which suggests the emotion they are conveying is not the same as the one they are genuinely feeling. These hidden emotional behaviors indicate a person is feeling insecure or is trying to hide their real feelings, which could also indicate something is potentially wrong.

Fourth Step: Baseline

Following a few minutes of observation, and interaction if it is appropriate, you must cultivate your baseline for that person. At this point, you are going to rapidly put together their physical, emotional, and verbal cues to make an assumption about what personality archetype this person is and what they are presently feeling. You will also make an assumption about what they need and what they are doing in order to fulfill that need.

Your baseline is not necessarily an accurate assumption, especially at first, so you need to be careful not to behave as though it is absolutely correct. Instead, use it as a foundation upon which to gather information and use it to either reinforce or contradict the assumptions you have made. As you continue to interact with that person, continue building out your baseline, so it is more complex and accommodates for more of their personality, such as their emotional reactions to different triggers.

Fifth Step: Deviations

After you have cultivated a baseline understanding of someone's emotions, you can start recognizing anytime they deviate away from it. Paying attention to deviations should happen only after you have a significant, confident grasp on their baseline, as this ensures you have a more accurate representation of who they are. Once you are confident in their baseline, you can start paying attention to deviations.

Deviations will show up in a person's significantly changed emotional and behavioral response to someone. If someone that has been generally calm suddenly becomes irate, for example, you know they have deviated away from their baseline. Deviations indicate how a person is feeling and, if you are trying to elicit a certain response or reaction out of them, can help you determine whether you are on the right track or not.

CHAPTER 17
Make Your Guess And Validate It

Regardless of what form of communication you are using with someone, you can guarantee that you two will never be exactly on the same page. Communication is a tricky skill, which we all interpret and experience in our own ways, making it even more challenging. Still, you must start somewhere, and the best place to start is by making a guess and then later validating it. "Guesstimating," as it is often called, means taking early cues from someone and using them to formulate an assumption of who you think a person is, how you think they behave, what they value, what they want, and how you can help them.

You will rapidly recognize that, despite how best your guesstimating is, people will always surprise you. Part of human nature is that we are all so unique that no amount of profiling can ever exactly define who we are. For that reason, people must guess and will always be both right and wrong, as they will only ever get to know the parts of us that we let them into.

Fortunately, analyzing a person to the point where you can interpret them accurately enough is all you need. You do not need to know the exact ins and outs of a person, or who they are, specifically. As long as you have an understanding of their values, desires, likes, and dislikes, and what their personality is like, you know enough.

Creating Your Original Personality Guess

Creating your original personality guess is a lot like creating your baseline understanding of a person. At this point, you want to profile them into a personality archetype so you have a clearer understanding of them. Personality archetypes are especially useful because they provide you with insight into a person's core driving factors, goals, fears, strengths, weaknesses, and potential. Understanding this information about someone means you can connect with them over things they care about and create a closer relationship with them based on this knowledge.

You can create your original personality guess by focusing on three cues: their energy, their words, and their mannerisms. Each of the 12 archetypes has a unique form of energy that determines how exuberant or outgoing they are or are not. Their words will also indicate whether they value humor, caretaking, heroism, or other such characteristics of the archetypes. Lastly, their mannerisms or how they carry themselves will provide you with something to work from, too. Look to see what topics they bring up, what types of questions they ask, and where they place their energy. The more you understand these, the easier it is for you to make accurate determinations of what a person's personality is like.

Be careful not to overthink your original personality archetype guess. Let your intuition guide you, and use your gut feeling combined with some of what you have observed from the person you are guessing for. Overthinking this initial judgment can make the entire process seemingly impossible because you fail to lay the foundation upon which you will make your official analysis. This is merely a starting point and a guiding factor in finding the true answer to which personality type each person has.

Validating Your Guess With Reinforcements

Once you have made your observation, begin to guess their archetype using reinforcements to validate your initial guess. Validation can be achieved in many ways, ranging from manipulating the situation to observing that person in different circumstances. Your overall goal is to decide whether each behavior reinforces, or contradicts, your assumption about what that person's archetype is. You might find that your initial assumption was correct, so now you gain greater context around your assumption and the true manifestation of that archetype in that individual. Or, you might find that your initial assumption was incorrect, and you were misinterpreting signals that were indicative of their true archetype. Or, perhaps, you positively interpreted symbols of their secondary archetype.

Remember that upon initially meeting someone, they will often behave differently. Even if they have no reason to, we all have an inner desire to impress others or hide from others if we are uncomfortable with that situation. The way a person presents themselves right away might not be accurate to their overall archetype but may instead be indicative of their secondary archetype. Either way, you can use their ongoing behavior to either reinforce, contradict, or clarify your assumptions about them and their behavior.

Manipulating The Situation For Validation

An excellent way to validate your assumption of someone's behavior is to observe them and the way they behave in many different situations. If you have plenty of time to spend with someone, you can let many or all of these situations occur organically through your interaction with this person. If, however, you have limited time or the circumstances you are in prevent you from fully exploring their personality, you may need to manipulate the situation.

The easiest way to manipulate the situation for validation on your initial assumption is to guide the conversation. Talk about many different things with enthusiasm, and see how the person you are communicating with responds. What topics do they bring up? What do they seem to value? What is their tonality like? Are they agreeing or disagreeing with you? Do they seem authentic in their answer, or are they saying it just to please you? All of these answers will allow you to identify whether you are accurately interpreting a situation or not.

Another way to manipulate the situation is to intentionally put yourself in specific circumstances with someone, so you can identify how they react. For example, you might intentionally take a date to your favorite restaurant, without telling them, to find out if they genuinely like the same foods you like. These types of manipulations merely manipulate the circumstances to create an opportunity for observation and should not be used to manipulate the other person. In doing so, you would lose your accurate analysis of them and have to interpret them in another way.

Looking For External Clues To Validate

External clues are an excellent way of validating your assumptions about someone and their personality. By external validations, I mean look for clues in the way they dress, the places they hang out at, who their friends are, and the way they physically interact with the world around them. Notice how they handle things, what their movements are like, and where they tend to spend most of their time.

If they are hanging out with a group of friends, are they in the center talking to everyone, or standing to the side with one or two other people, or alone entirely? At work, do they walk directly where they need to go, or do they stop and chat with people along the way? Are they a generally clean person, or do they keep their spaces messy?

This external information is a great way to validate whether you are accurate or inaccurate with your findings. The environments people spend time in, the way they carry themselves, and the methods they use for interacting with their environment and surroundings are all indicative of who they are. You can learn a lot about a person's values, preferences, and beliefs by their surroundings. Each of these perfectly works toward describing that person's personality to you, too.

Asking For Validation Outright

In some scenarios, asking for validation outright may be a perfectly acceptable way of identifying someone's personality. In doing so, you must either casually inject your questions into the conversation or ask them during times when it would be appropriate to ask such a thing.

When you are casually injecting things into a conversation, consider looking for organic ways to ask. For example, when someone tells you something about yourself, say, "Oh! You are quite outgoing, are you?" This is an excellent way to interject these questions, without directly asking someone something rather personal about themselves. Further, most people are unaware of their personality type or may be offended by it, so asking for exacting personality types is not recommended. Instead, ask questions that give you some insight into the characteristics that the person has, which allows you to profile them into an archetype on your own.

If you are in a situation where asking such questions is natural or expected in the conversation, you can always ask outright and with seriousness. For example, in an interview or on an early date with someone new, you might ask, "What would you describe your personality type as?" This may seem like a dry or overused question; however, it does get directly to the point. It is worth noting that the personality archetype that someone declares they have may not be accurate, or it may not be the personality type you see out of them. Often, people view themselves differently than others do, and people show up differently in the many relationships in their lives, which can make getting an exact representation challenging. It is wise to use this as a piece of the overall assumption you make, rather than the assumption itself. Continue to observe for clues of an accurate interpretation, and use that to help you make your dynamic view of each person.

CHAPTER 18
Be Flexible In Your Understanding

Reading body language can provide you with fairly accurate interpretations of others, though it can never give you exact interpretations. While reading body language is often accurate and gives you plenty of information to go from when it comes to communicating with others, you must understand that you can easily make mistakes while reading this form of communication. Beyond body language, facial expressions, tones, words, and even full messages can be misinterpreted by you, making your ability to fully and accurately analyze a human rather challenging.

The best thing to remember is that you do not need to be 100% accurate in order to gain enough information from body language to use it to your advantage. If you do not remain flexible in your understanding, you run the risk of holding people to inaccurate images, misinterpreting them, or even carrying lifelong opinions of them that are irrelevant to who they really are. Always be flexible in your interpretation of others', and be willing to adapt your interpretation to new information you receive. This way, you always have an accurate representation of people, which makes interacting and connecting with them far more efficient.

Your Mood May Project Onto Others

One of the most significant reasons why your analysis of another person may be incorrect is because you are projecting onto others. Projections are most likely when we make an assumption about someone else based on what we would feel, think, or do in those circumstances. If they behave as we do, we assume they are just like us. If they don't, we assume they are just like someone that we know that they *are* similar to. You might use this information to unfairly judge someone or categorize them based on how another person is, and not they themselves.

Even if you are not generally the type to project onto others, you might find yourself projecting based on a mood you are in or the way you are feeling. These temporary emotional states can lead to our perspective of the world around us, shifting, which can impact our ability to analyze others. Always be sure to check yourself and your mood before analyzing others to ensure you remain objective in your observations. If you find you cannot reasonably tell the difference, avoid trying to analyze anyone as you might create unfair first interpretations, which can be challenging to revise at a later date.

Your Judgment May Be Clouded

Your judgment can easily become clouded by other people and unusual circumstances if you are not careful. Clouded judgment can lead to you making false or unfair assumptions about people or possibly misinterpreting them altogether because you failed to remain objective in your observation. The most common reason to have clouded judgment is that you made an assumption about a person before you had enough information to do so. If you find yourself in the habit of feeling as though you already know someone before you have even talked to them, you are robbing yourself of the opportunity to actually know and understand other people. You must communicate with someone and interact with them first before making your assumption; otherwise, you will lack essential information for your analysis.

The most likely ways to prejudge someone include judging them by their looks, listening to gossip or rumors that were being spread about them, or judging them based on the way they behaved in one isolated incident. If you have made a judgment about anyone based on this information, it is worth it to revisit your judgment and consider that it may be inaccurate. With an open mind, review your assumption and look for new evidence to validate or contradict it without leaning into cognitive bias.

That Person May Be Behaving Differently

One especially important reason to remain flexible when gauging people's personalities is that they may be behaving differently than they normally would, which would interrupt your ability to accurately judge them. If you meet or are interacting with someone during a time when they are behaving differently than how they normally would, you will not get to know who they really are. If you do not already know someone and they behave in a way that is off-putting, it may be worthwhile to assume this was just a mood they were in and to give them a second chance. If, after that second chance, they continue to behave the same way, then you can assume this is their personality.

One small factor you can look at that might indicate an overall personality trait, rather than a mood-related behavior, is how they seem to act about things unrelated to the topic they are reacting to. For example, let's say a customer comes into your store behaving erratically because they are angry with something they have experienced. If their spouse called and they had to answer, listening to the way they addressed their partner while angry would be a great way to determine if they were more aggressive overall or if their anger was isolated to the present experience. This same approach can be applied to any number of situations to determine someone's likely overall personality on occasions where you do not have a lot of time to get to know it otherwise.

You May Have Misinterpreted Your Gut

Your gut feeling about a person will virtually always be right, but you may have misinterpreted the messages your gut was giving you. People often misinterpret these messages when they find themselves in circumstances that feel too familiar, especially if it is a negative familiar. For example, if you have a trauma or a bad memory from a specific circumstance, you might misinterpret people or their behaviors when you are with them in a similar circumstance because you have emotional flashbacks. These emotional flashbacks can be strong enough to prevent you from accurately interpreting other people because you are viewing them through a heavily biased lens.

It is important to remember that, despite the similarities that exist between people and circumstances throughout our lives, no two people are the same; therefore, the experiences you have with different people will always turn out differently. If you find yourself experiencing emotional triggers and misinterpreting signals someone is giving you, assume that your gut instinct is being falsely interpreted, or triggered, and look for other clues to learn more about that person. Otherwise, do not overthink your gut, and trust what it has to say.

You May Have Over Thought It

Overthinking can sabotage many things, including your ability to analyze people. Your initial analysis of someone will include recent judgments based on their actions, words, behaviors, and other cues you picked up on during your communications. At the time of you making these assumptions, your answers were most likely to be accurate. The trouble with overthinking things is that, while doing it, you genuinely believe you are not overthinking something; rather, you are "realizing after the fact" that you likely interpreted it wrong. This is rooted in insecurity, not a genuine change of heart in your gut feeling. Be wary of this behavior.

There is one reliable way to determine if you are overthinking something or if you genuinely misjudged something. If you are agonizing over something and playing it over and over in your mind, trying to determine if you accurately interpreted something, you are overthinking it. You repetitively recalling the event will actually change your memory of the event, therefore giving you an inaccurate interpretation of it. Never change your mind once you have made it up *unless* you gain reliable new information that is worth changing your mind over. For example, if you meet with that person again and their new behavior contradicts your initial interpretation, now it is worth it to re-analyze and reconsider your initial assumption. Otherwise, you are likely overthinking it!

CONCLUSION

Congratulations on completing *How To Analyze People!*

Knowing how to accurately analyze people is an imperative part of anyone's life. From everyday communication to conducting business dealings or meeting new people, knowing how to analyze other people is a significantly useful life skill. Through your accurate ability to analyze people, you gain the ability to recognize their characteristics, understand their personality, identify their likes and dislikes, and connect with them in a way that feels good to them.

As you continue to practice analyzing people, you will discover that your understanding of different cues and signs grows. Seeing different behaviors in the flesh provides a level of context that cannot be gained in reading, as you are able to interpret these signals through the tangible senses of your body. Continue analyzing people in as many situations as possible to refine your interpretation of these signals, as this will allow you to deepen your innate knowledge of people and conduct more accurate analysis.

When it comes to using your analysis, you must remember to always use it for the genuine good of everyone. Use it to better understand people, connect with them in a more positive way, and support them throughout their life. Never feel as though you have to manipulate other people, even if you think those manipulations will create more positive in their lives. You are not obligated to people-please, nor are you obligated to use this information to take better care of others. On the contrary, you should use this information to help you relate better with people while connecting with them on an individual level in a more meaningful way.

If you have chosen to explore human analysis for a unique purpose, it is best to practice using it in that area of your life as often as you can. The more you use it in this area of your life, the better you will be at interpreting signs and using them to your desired advantage. Know, too, that what you learn in this area of your life will serve in other areas, as once you know how to interpret body language in one way, it becomes a lot easier to do it in other ways, as well.

The next step you should take after reading this book is to begin getting serious about analyzing others but also learning to analyze yourself. Whenever you can, get into observation mode and observe what your natural interactions are like. Your interactions will naturally shift as you are now paying such close attention to them; however, you will still get the opportunity to see how you generally behave, or what feels natural for you. Observing your own behavior is excellent because it gives you the opportunity to express yourself more intentionally around others, thus creating the image you desire to create with them. Further, it gives you the opportunity to understand yourself better and help yourself grow in whatever direction you desire.

Whether you were here for a reason, or you were here to simply learn more about people and the world around you, I want to thank you for reading *How To Analyze People*. I hope you learned plenty about human analysis and are feeling confident in your ability to interpret and understand people as you need to.

Before you go, I ask that you please take a moment to honestly review *How To Analyze People* on Amazon. Your feedback would be greatly appreciated, as it allows others to discover this title and use it to support their own understanding of people. Further, it allows me to understand how you enjoyed this title, so I can create more great content for you!

Thank you, and best of luck with analyzing people. Remember, trust your gut, and stay flexible! You might be surprised to discover what you learn about people, the more open you remain.

DESCRIPTION

Human analysis is a natural part of our everyday lives, yet very few people genuinely understand what it is or know how to consciously read the cues other people are giving them. If you find yourself constantly overthinking people's behaviors, analyzing people's voices, and feeling insecure or uncertain around their cues, you need to learn more about human analysis.

The process of analyzing people is relevant to countless areas of your life. From a primal and biological perspective, human analysis enables you to feel confident that you are not surrounded by someone that is dangerous, or who could become dangerous at any point in the future. In more modern ways, human analysis can help you trust people, make sales, get to know your date, connect with friends and family, feel more confident around people, enjoy healthier connections with others, or even get to know yourself better.

Despite the fact that your subconscious brain already knows how to analyze people, your conscious brain may have no idea. By reading *How To Analyze People,* you will uncover excellent strategies for bringing your conscious awareness on board with analyzing people, so you feel more confident in your interpretations. Further, you can use this information strategically to improve your ability to connect with or work with others. This book provides you with excellent, in-depth guidance for analyzing people, leaving no questions unanswered. You will discover countless techniques that allow you to make quick, efficient, and meaningful assumptions, and to validate those assumptions, so your findings are accurate.

Some of the specific topics we cover in *How To Analyze People* include:
- Why you should analyze people and the various methods for getting started
- The importance of body language and how to read someone's body
- Facial expressions and the necessary steps for reading micro-expressions
- What someone's eyes say about them, and how to interpret eye movement like an FBI agent
- How your intuition plays into reading people and analyzing their behaviors
- What emotional energy is and how to read it on people
- How to identify someone's baseline and observe their deviations (and why)
- The meaning of phrases like cluster gestures and mirrored behavior, and why it matters to you

- How to put the reading together, make an educated guess, and validate it
- The importance of staying flexible to learn as much as possible
- And more!

By following the step-by-step guide for reading someone's behavior that is detailed within this book, and including the many additional nuances we discuss, you will discover exactly how to accurately analyze people. Understand that it will take practice on your behalf to put context to what you are taught, but with this book, you can read anyone with ease and confidence.

Discover how to stop overthinking and overanalyzing, and start clearly understanding people today! Purchase *How To Analyze People* and uncover the unique, hidden languages of humankind, and how these languages can be used to communicate both consciously and subconsciously with other people. You won't be disappointed that you did!

www.ingramcontent.com/pod-product-compliance
Lightning Source LLC
Chambersburg PA
CBHW071451070526
44578CB00001B/309